Activities for including children with

Behavioural difficulties

MANAGING DIFFICULT BEHAVIOUR • PRACTICAL ACTIVITIES • ASSESSMENT ADVICE • COVERS AD/HD & AGGRESSION

DR HANNAH MORTIMER
LOUISE CARRUTHERS AND HELEN LANE

Authors
Dr Hannah Mortimer, Louise Carruthers and Helen Lane

Editor
Victoria Lee

Assistant Editor
Anna Avino

Series Designers
Sarah Rock/Anna Oliwa

Designer
Andrea Lewis

Illustrations
Debbie Clark

Cover artwork
Richard Johnson

Text © 2004, Hannah Mortimer
© 2004, Scholastic Ltd

Designed using Adobe InDesign

Published by Scholastic Ltd, Villiers House,
Clarendon Avenue, Leamington Spa, Warwickshire CV32 5PR

Visit our website at www.scholastic.co.uk

Printed by Bell & Bain Ltd, Glasgow

1 2 3 4 5 6 7 8 9 0   4 5 6 7 8 9 0 1 2 3

British Library Cataloguing-in-Publication Data A catalogue record for this book is available from the British Library.

ISBN 0 439 971632

Activities for including children with behavioural difficulties

INTRODUCTION

Including children with behavioural, social and emotional difficulties can be very challenging. This book aims to help you strike the best balance so that all the children progress.

Aims of the series

There is a revised *Code of Practice* in England for the identification and assessment of special educational needs that has been published by the DfES and also new guidance on including children who have disabilities. In addition, the National Numeracy and National Literacy Strategies emphasise the key role that teachers play in making sure that the curriculum is accessible to all pupils. The Government's strategy for special educational needs (SEN) includes a whole framework of initiatives to remove barriers to pupils' achievement and we are now beginning to see joined up policies that can make real differences to children. This series aims to provide suggestions to class teachers and others working in schools on how to meet and monitor SEN under the new guidelines. It will provide accessible information and advice for teachers at Key Stage 1 and Key Stage 2. It will also provide practical examples of how they can use this information to plan inclusive teaching across the strands of the National Curriculum.

There is related legislation and guidance in Wales, Scotland and Northern Ireland though the detail and terminology are rather different. For example, the Statement of SEN in England and Wales is called a Record in Scotland. Nevertheless, the general approaches and information covered in this book will be relevant throughout the UK.

Within this *Special Needs in the Primary Years* series, there are three books on helping children with most kinds of special need:
● *Special Needs Handbook*, which supplies general information for SENCOs or class teachers to help meet all the special educational needs in the school or class.
● *Complete Guide to Special Needs from A–Z*, which provides basic information for class teachers and support assistants.
● *Activities for Including Children with Behavioural Difficulties*, which suggests a range of practical activities for including these children in the primary curriculum.

Including children with behavioural difficulties

All classes will at some point include children who have behavioural and emotional difficulties. While teachers are encouraged to include these children, in practice this can be a challenge. Teachers may recognise the need for inclusion but find it hard to strike the right balance between meeting a child's individual needs and ensuring that the progress of the other children is not disrupted. This book aims to provide a broad understanding of different areas of behavioural and emotional difficulty and show how primary teachers can make individual behaviour plans for these children.

You need to make sure that the child with behavioural difficulties is accessing the full range of your educational provision. Clearly this cannot happen if the child is isolated in any way or withdrawn from the group regularly, and this is another reason for collecting ideas for inclusive group activities. Support does not mean individual one-to-one attention. Instead, it can mean playing alongside a child or watching on so as to encourage positive behaviour, staying 'one step ahead' of any problem times, adopting positive strategies for managing inappropriate behaviour and teaching the child social skills in small groups.

Who this book is for

First and foremost, this book is for special educational needs co-ordinators (SENCOs), class teachers and support assistants who work on a daily basis with children. The book will also be helpful for support professionals, head teachers and governors to use with the staff they work with. Finally, the book will be a useful reference for parents, carers and trainees.

Children can demonstrate behavioural and emotional difficulties for a range of reasons and this book aims to cover the most common: children whose behaviour is challenging, children who are shy and slow to settle, children who have difficulties attending and concentrating, and children who have been emotionally affected by major life changes (such as family separation and bereavement).

How to use this book

In Chapter 1 you will be introduced to the concept of 'inclusion' as it relates to children with behavioural and emotional difficulties. In particular, you will see what the implications of these difficulties are for the child and for the teacher at different ages and stages. You will also think about some of the issues and challenges that you face when working with these children. There are suggestions for assessing children with different kinds of behavioural difficulties in Chapter 2. Each type of difficulty might call for a different kind of assessment and you will be helped to select the most appropriate method for your situation. You will also find a description of the legal requirements on you to identify and support children who have SEN on account of their behavioural or emotional difficulties. Chapter 3 helps you to plan interventions for these children, working with their strengths and weaknesses. In this chapter you will find a wide range of approaches which colleagues in other schools have found helpful and you will later be helped to match these approaches effectively to your teaching activities.

Six activity chapters follow and these cover the six strands of the National Curriculum which are perhaps affected most by this area of need. If a child has a significant difficulty in concentrating, settling to work and maintaining attention, then most will experience learning difficulties in the areas of English 1: Speaking and listening, and English 3: Writing. Children who find it difficult to behave may have particular difficulties in the less structured or more practical activities, such as Design and technology, Art and design, Music and PE where the boundaries on their behaviour are less clear. Though there may well be learning difficulties across each area of the curriculum, it is hoped that the examples in these six areas will provide you with the starting points and ideas necessary for helping you deliver the entire curriculum in a supportive and inclusive way. There are two teaching activities for each age range of five to seven years, seven to nine years and nine to eleven years, each on a separate page. You will also find an introduction to each strand, covering how children with behavioural and emotional difficulties are likely to be affected in that particular area of the curriculum. This links back to Chapter 2 and allows you to select the most appropriate methods of assessment and observation for that area of the curriculum.

For each teaching activity, you will find a 'Learning Objective for all the children' and also an 'Individual behaviour target' for children with behavioural difficulties. There are also suggestions for providing 'Special support' and for 'Extension' (what to try next for the children if the target was met). The support suggestions link back to Chapter 3 where each approach is described to you in more detail. The activities have been selected to make a particular point for teaching children with behavioural and emotional difficulties, reflecting the strengths, weaknesses, opportunities and challenges of those pupils. They should be adapted to suit the situation of each teacher and class and should act as a stimulus to trigger ideas and for the teacher to adapt. Throughout the book there are photocopiable pages linked to behaviour assessment, monitoring and planning the activities and, at the end of the book, there is a list of helpful resources. You will find more detail about meeting SEN in the book *Special Needs Handbook* by Hannah Mortimer (Scholastic), also from this series.

Setting the scene

The activities described in this book encourage you to make use of a wide range of resources available in your school. Special use is made of circle-time approaches since these have been shown to be very effective in building children's self-esteem and confidence and in teaching them how to behave in a group. Confidence and learning seem to be bound together; if a child tries something and succeeds, self-esteem and confidence are raised and they are likely to try again next time and to learn. On the other hand, if a child tries something but cannot succeed, self-esteem and confidence are lowered and they are less likely to try again. That is why it is so important that the approaches we design for helping children's behaviour and social development to change should remain positive and should leave the children feeling good about themselves.

In just the same way, as staff members, you need to be confident if you are to cope with the various challenging behaviours you will meet in your school. The learning activities you plan should involve strategies for managing challenging behaviour that are workable and effective and should leave staff and children alike feeling positive. That is why this book has been written around a framework of inclusive classroom activities as well as a theoretical understanding of why children behave in the way that they do (covered in Chapter 1).

If you skim through the entire book first, focusing especially on the curriculum introductions and on the ideas for support, you will pick up ideas which you can transfer to different situations and different curriculum areas. After that, you may find it best to dip into the book as necessary, using it as flexibly as you need to.

The children concerned

Not all children who have behavioural or emotional difficulties have boisterous and challenging behaviour – you should be just as concerned about the child who is very quiet, withdrawn or whose behaviour changes suddenly . Children can show emotional difficulties for many different reasons. Some of these will stem from their past, their life changes or their relationships with others. In the first chapter, you will read about some of the risk factors that make children vulnerable to emotional and behavioural difficulties and to mental health problems. You need to have a basic awareness of the risk factors associated with abuse, whether it is physical, emotional or sexual. The need to act on any concerns about child protection override all the suggestions in this book and must always take priority, however difficult it may be at the time. You also need to have in mind your own safety at all times and there are some general pointers throughout the book for ensuring your own health and safety as well.

Links with home

The revised SEN *Code of Practice* has strengthened the importance of 'parent partnership' and of good communication and joint planning between school and home. Sometimes a child's behavioural and emotional difficulties are such that you need to place their names on the school's SEN register and take School Action, setting and reviewing a regular individual behaviour plan. In this case, you are obliged to involve parents and carers fully in the process. It is not always easy talking to parents and carers about their child's behaviour and you may find this easier if you can share some of the activities and approaches you are doing in class, discussing the ideas for target setting, support and extension which are exemplified in this book. The SEN review system to be adopted when a child's behaviour appears to need additional or different approaches to the usual ones is described fully in the *Special Needs Handbook* by Hannah Mortimer (Scholastic).

Overview grid for ages 5–7

ACTIVITY TITLE	SUBJECT	BEHAVIOUR TARGET	LEARNING OBJECTIVE	OUTCOME
PUPPET INVITATIONS	Writing	To concentrate on a written activity for ten minutes.	To write a letter of invitation.	A letter inviting a lonely puppet to come and stay that encourages reluctant writers to do their best.
DRIVE AND WRITE	Writing	To learn how to form letters correctly.	To learn how to form the letter 'O' correctly.	A multi-sensory approach to letter formation involving making circular tracks.
TREASURE HUNT	Speaking and listening	To be motivated enough to work, join in and behave appropriately for a whole activity.	To listen carefully to and remember simple instructions. To communicate simple instructions to a small group of children.	A navigating game with a pirate treasure map, involving group co-operation and direction vocabulary.
LUCKY DIP!	Speaking and listening	To share and take turns in a small group.	To use appropriate vocabulary when describing details to others.	A circle game in which children take turns to be listeners or describers.
IN THE PICTURE	Design and technology	To handle small tools safely.	To use scissors and hole-punches with care and control.	An activity in which the children make a personalised photograph frame with simple tools.
CHOCOLATE CHALLENGE	Design and technology	To try again if they do not succeed first time.	To assemble reclaimed materials to make a wheeled vehicle for a specific purpose. To gain some understanding of how wheels and axles work.	Children are challenged to make a chocolate transporter out of junk material.
MUSICAL PRINTS	Art and design	To be happy to join in and pleased with their efforts.	To use a simple painting technique to represent the feelings evoked by a piece of music.	Children listen to music and create colourful and sensory artwork to represent their feelings.
CLAY TILES	Art and design	To make a simple plan and see it through.	To design and make a clay tile. To use a range of tools to create different print effects.	Persistence is encouraged in this activity in which children make their own clay tiles.
ALL PLAY!	Music	To join in appropriately with a group activity.	To understand and respond to the terms 'fast', 'slow' and 'stop'. To listen carefully and identify changes in tempo.	A circle game with dice in which children take turns to join in with simple rhythms.
ANIMAL HULLABALOO	Music	To pay attention and stay 'on task' for the whole lesson.	To rehearse and perform a simple musical pattern in a small group.	Distractible children are helped to focus in this activity with percussion instruments and an animal song.
AS QUIET AS MICE	PE	To become physically active without becoming angry or overexcited.	To show an awareness of space and other children when playing a simple team game.	Children pretend to be mice and move quickly and quietly to avoid the cat!
UNDERWATER PATTERNS	PE	To be confident enough to perform a linked sequence of movements in front of a large group.	To copy, remember and repeat simple actions with control and co-ordination. To create and perform a short sequence of actions with a partner.	Children learn to move in different ways to represent a variety of sea creatures.

Overview grid for ages 7–9

ACTIVITY TITLE	SUBJECT	BEHAVIOUR TARGET	LEARNING OBJECTIVE	OUTCOME
TIMELINES	Writing	To write about how they feel.	To plot events on a timeline.	Using timelines to help children talk about their life events and feelings.
SCHOOL–TRIP LETTERS	Writing	To use writing to achieve an end.	To write a letter requesting information.	Reluctant writers are encouraged to write a real letter organising an outing.
DRAW A STORY	Speaking and listening	To listen and respond appropriately for ten minutes.	To retell a story.	Children listen to a story, illustrate it section by section, and then retell the whole story to a partner.
LISTENING GAMES	Speaking and listening	To remember and repeat a sentence.	To listen and respond using appropriate reasoning.	Simple sentence building, questioning and memory games to help children focus their attention.
POP UP CARDS	Design and technology	To develop a workable idea and see it through.	To design and make a pop-up card. (Cross curricula link to Maths: symmetry).	A motivating activity involving following a sequence of instructions and evaluating the product.
WISH BOXES	Design and technology	To look at their work objectively, improve it and provide constructive criticism to others.	To produce a box using a net. This can be linked to QCA teaching units Design and technology 3a packages, and Maths for realising 3-D shapes from 2-D images.	Children work in pairs to create a 3-D box to contain their personal wishes.
THROUGH THE VIEWFINDER	Art and design	To remain focused on a visual task and become absorbed in the process.	To observe small details from a larger visual stimulus. This can be linked in particular to QCA teaching units 3b Investigating pattern and 4a Viewpoints (about dreams).	Children use a viewfinder to study and draw fine detail, evaluating their techniques with each other.
PAINT FACTORY	Art and design	To express feelings through paint and talk about these to a teacher.	To mix paint colours together producing new colours and shades.	An activity that involves talking about feelings and creating a unique and personal paint mix.
CARNIVAL OF THE ANIMALS	Music	To take part in the lesson without becoming angry, anxious or excited.	To identify how music can be used descriptively (for example to represent different animal characters).	The music is used as a stimulus for talking about and sketching different animals.
RHYTHM PATTERNS	Music	To work co-operatively in a small group.	To distinguish and clap syllables and to put a sequence of rhythm patterns together.	Coloured cards are used to signal different rhythms that the children then use in their own compositions.
BASKETBALL	PE	To find a space and not to invade the space of others.	To use the tactic of finding space in a competitive game.	This motivating sport provides opportunities for practising skills and discussing rules.
RELAXATION GAMES	PE	To learn a simple relaxation technique.	To know and understand their own bodies.	Two activities to help children relax their bodies and minds, also useful in anger and stress management techniques.

Overview grid for ages 9–11

ACTIVITY TITLE	SUBJECT	BEHAVIOUR TARGET	LEARNING OBJECTIVE	OUTCOME
PAPER AEROPLANES	Writing	To write a paragraph of information independently.	To write an instructional text.	Children attempt to provide clear instructions for their partners to make a paper aeroplane and discuss how to improve on them.
BEING BULLIED?	Writing	To use writing to express feelings about bullying.	To write an account of an imaginary event.	Children talk and write about bullying and discuss the feelings involved.
CELEBRITY INTERVIEWS	Speaking and listening	To work calmly and productively alongside others.	To empathise with another person, assuming their character. To ask questions and gather biographical information on another person.	Children use an interview schedule and consider what it would be like to be famous.
FLASHBACKS AND FLASH FORWARDS	Speaking and listening	To speak confidently in front of a large group.	To devise a short role-play based on given characters.	Different scenarios are used to help children discuss the antecedents and consequences of behaviour.
MAKING BREAD	Design and technology	To learn and concentrate on a complex practical task.	To accurately follow a recipe for bread making. Link to Design and technology unit 5b.	Children follow baking instructions carefully, step by small step, in order to produce a tasty result.
COMFORT CUSHIONS	Design and technology	To develop methods of calming themselves when angry, tense or anxious.	To design and make a patchwork cushion. Covering programmes of study 3a, 3b, 4b, 4c and aspects of 2a and 2c.	Children create a personal and calming cushion made from pleasing textures and coloured fabrics.
CARTOON FLIPBOOKS	Art and design	To complete a piece of art based on a topic of personal interest.	To produce a flipbook showing movement. Link to Art QCA 6a, People in action.	Children have to work carefully and accurately to produce this rewarding product.
THE ROLE OF AN ARTIST	Art and design	To use IT appropriately and to remain focused.	To investigate the roles of artists, crafts people and designers working in different times and different cultures.	Children use websites to research the role of artists and share their findings as a group.
COMPUTER COMPOSITION	Music	To work independently on a given task, asking for help when appropriate.	To compose a piece of music.	A computer programme is used to help children generate their own musical compositions.
PERFORMANCE POETRY	Music	To contribute new ideas with confidence.	To add music and percussion to poetry and then perform.	Favourite poetry is used to inspire the children to compose musical accompaniments.
FAST GAMES	PE	To move safely at speed.	To understand and participate in group games effectively.	Two motivating and simple games to help the children develop speed and safe control when moving.
CIRCUIT TRAINING	PE	To become self-motivated to exercise regularly.	To self-record performance and to set personal targets for the future.	Children are set several challenges and encouraged to improve on their personal best performances.

UNDERSTANDING BEHAVIOURAL DIFFICULTIES

In this chapter you will think about why behavioural and emotional difficulties are often linked and why it is important to plan approaches to help pupils avoid mental health problems.

In addition to the above, the effect that low self-esteem and poor confidence can play on learning and behaviour is explained in this chapter. All of these factors will help you to see how important it is to plan behavioural interventions that are 'positive'. You will then meet a range of common behaviour difficulties shown by five- to seven-year-olds and seven- to eleven-year-olds. All of these behaviours will be revisited in Chapter 2 when you consider observation and assessment, and in Chapter 3 when you think about interventions.

Since this is a book about special educational needs, the explanations, methods of assessment and interventions are all based on the assumption that a child needs something *additional and different* to the usual approach. In other words, *all* children sometimes tell fibs, act aggressively or seek attention. You do not need to resort to additional and different approaches to manage this very normal kind of day-to-day behaviour. However, when a child is displaying the behaviour in an exaggerated way, when it has persisted for a long time despite your usual interventions, or when it is seriously affecting the other children, then you will need to plan an individual approach.

Why we link behaviour and emotional difficulties

The document 'Promoting Children's Mental Health within Early Years and School Settings' (DfES) provides guidance for LEAs, schools, early years settings and child and adolescent mental health services. It starts by defining 'mental health' as the ability to:

- develop psychologically, emotionally, intellectually and spiritually
- initiate, develop and sustain mutually satisfying relationships
- use and enjoy solitude
- become aware of others and empathise with them
- play and learn
- develop a sense of right and wrong
- resolve (or face) problems and setbacks and learn from them.

It goes on to describe the types of mental health problems experienced by children, such as 'attachment disorders' or 'conduct disorders', and links these back to the term 'emotional and behavioural difficulties', suggesting that the one has a greater risk of leading to the other. It stresses the link between children's emotional well-being and learning well. In other words, if you can take steps to make sure that children's mental health is as strong as possible during their childhoods, then you actually have a chance of reducing

the behavioural and emotional difficulties in your school. Clearly there is only so much you can do in school, but the move now is towards cross-agency joined-up working so that everybody can tackle these issues together in community, home and education.

Risk factors

The more that you find out about mental health, the more possible it becomes to identify certain children who are *at risk* of developing problems later on in life because of their particular childhood experiences and predispositions. We now know that the more the risk factors, and the more severe the risks, the more likely the child is to develop a mental health problem later on. There is also research that suggests that, unless steps are taken to counteract this, depression and mental illness will soon cause more days off work than any other illness. It is so important that you begin to recognise behavioural difficulties as behaviours that certain children display because of their particular life experiences, rather than labelling the children as difficult and demanding.

There are a number of risk factors for children making them more likely to experience behavioural difficulties or mental health problems later on. These are:
● loss or separation, perhaps because someone in the family has died, parents or carers have split up, there has been a long period in hospital or there have been many changes of home and carers
● major life changes, such as becoming a refugee, moving house or changing families ('looked after' children are particularly vulnerable)
● traumatic events, such as violence, accidents, injuries, war, natural disaster or abuse
● having a 'difficult temperament' or a very low self-esteem, perhaps not being flexible enough to adapt to different social situations
● having learning or communication difficulties
● socio-economic disadvantage and homelessness.

While many children with many of these risk factors will grow and develop with no mental health problems whatsoever, risk factors do seem to 'stack' up.

Avoiding risk

It is also possible to identify certain *resilience factors* in children, families and communities which are going to make the children less likely to develop mental health problems later on. Again be aware of these so that you can build on what is known about avoiding risk. Children who may have these resilience factors are those who:
● enjoyed secure early relationships with their parents or carers
● were seen as 'easy' babies by their caregivers and who were therefore responded to with warmth
● have developed good ways of communicating with others
● have been brought up with humour, affection, care and optimism
● have parents and carers who support their education
● are from families where there is harmony and mutual support
● have good housing, a good standard of living and a positive ethos in the community.

While some of these factors will be hard to influence, you can see just how important it is that each and every child should develop a positive relationship with at least one caregiver and, where necessary, this can be within the school.

The importance of self-esteem

The term 'self-esteem' is usually used to mean that people have a favourable opinion of their own worth or 'are happy in their skins'. You can identify children whose self-esteem is low by observing and teaching them over a period of time. We all have good days and bad days, but in general children with low self-esteem:

- usually have a strong need for reassurance and praise from others
- feel insecure and lack trust in their ability to do things or to succeed
- have problems in trying out new experiences or in learning
- seem to expect things to go wrong for them and appear powerless to change this
- are reluctant to express ideas or make choices for themselves
- overreact to failure
- find it hard to accept correction without hostility or overreaction
- find it hard to accept praise
- seem not to trust others.

On the other hand, children who have high self-esteem:

- usually behave more appropriately
- are more willing to take risks when learning new things
- appear to be more confident
- are better motivated to try
- make friends more easily
- view other people positively
- can accept correction or suggestion without giving up
- develop a good sense of what they are good at and what they need help with.

Low self-esteem can be influenced by the ways in which adults behave towards children. For example, permissive caring and parenting styles in which children are allowed to behave how they wish actually lead to lower self-esteem. Children benefit more from clear boundaries and firm but caring structure. Children also do best where parents and teachers value the child as a contributor to daily life and decisions. Finally, children do best where explanation is used to control behaviour rather than enforcement. It seems that the best balance is where parents or teachers have the ultimate say in what a child does, but the child is offered *choices* within that boundary.

Creating the right ethos

If you accept that every child is entitled to opportunities to form respectful relationships with other children and adults and to be safe from emotional and physical harm, then ways of creating the right ethos develop naturally. Straight away, you can see how isolating a child or preventing them from learning alongside others is not as desirable as teaching the child how to behave appropriately. If you think about the entitlements of all children, then it is clear that all children need to be supported in their learning by staff who:

- work with parents and carers with trust, respecting each other's concerns, circumstances, practices and traditions
- are respectful of differences between individual children
- have high expectations of all children's developing capabilities, giving them opportunities to take risks, to experience success and failure, and to reflect on their own learning and achievements
- value them for their religious, ethnic, cultural, linguistic and gender identities, and for their special needs, aptitudes and interests
- sensitively extend the range of each child's responsibilities
- listen, watch, take time to understand, welcome children's questioning, follow where children lead, and provide time, space and opportunities for extending children's thinking, learning, imagining and understanding
- treat everyone with respect and equal concern.

Emotional intelligence

There is now a school of thought which claims that there are many different kinds of intelligences, all of which affect our abilities. It looks as though we all have different intelligences in dealing with *emotions* as well as with knowledge and reasoning and the term 'emotional intelligence' is used to describe this. It is a type of social intelligence that involves the ability to monitor one's own and other people's emotions, to discriminate among them, and to use the information to guide one's thinking and actions. Emotional intelligence is seen as involving self-awareness, the ability to manage emotions, self-motivation, empathy, and relationship skills. Some would argue that these intelligences are no more than social skills that can be taught or learned through experience. Others have argued that they are ways to perceive and regulate emotional thought and some people are better endowed than others.

In your school, you are probably aware that some children find it genuinely more difficult than others to understand social situations and handle emotions. An understanding of the child's strengths and weaknesses in Personal, social and emotional development should help you to plan approaches for these children. The term 'emotional literacy' is sometimes used to describe the work we can do with children to foster their mental health and emotional intelligence. It is helpful if you can see yourself as an educator of children's emotional literacy and not merely as a professional who has to deal with a range of difficult and challenging behaviours.

You need support too

Whenever you are working with particularly challenging behaviour in the children, your own self-esteem might be vulnerable as well, so you will need additional support from your peers and line managers. Look for chances of setting up peer support groups or consultation meetings with a manager or an outside professional so that you can feel confident in the approaches you are using. You might also need to take steps to manage your own stress at this difficult time. Make sure that there is space in your busy week for time to yourself with opportunities to meet with friends and pamper yourself a bit.

Appropriate behaviour

If you are going to speak of 'difficult' behaviours, it is helpful to be clear about appropriate behaviour you are hoping to encourage in the first place. It is probable that you would like children to:

● feel motivated and confident enough to reach their potential
● respect themselves and other people
● make friends and gain affection
● express their feelings in appropriate ways
● 'do as they are nicely asked'
● make a useful contribution to the class and school community
● develop positive self-esteem.

Guiding principles for managing difficult behaviour

● Encourage the children to behave appropriately using positive approaches that encourage their self-esteem.

● Manage the children's behaviour with proper respect for the children themselves and their parents or carers. Respect their culture, ethnicity, language, religion, age and gender. The approaches you use for managing behaviour must be respectful of all children regardless of their gifts, abilities or specific learning needs.

● Behaviour management and the personal, social and emotional education of children are not separate, discrete activities. As a consequence, when you work with young children's behaviour, you need to attend to their whole development and lives and not just to certain aspects of it.

● In your dealings with your pupils, aim for a 'caring use of power'. Teachers inevitably have power; this needs to be acknowledged and used caringly, respectfully, wisely and well.

● The interests of each child are paramount. Changing children's behaviour must enhance their lives, their learning and their development. It must work for the children concerned and it must work for the other children as well.

● You also need to recognise that children will thrive best only if their families thrive and you should work in close partnership with families and the community.

What the difficulties might mean for your situation

Here is a list of the most common behaviour problems in primary schools (as reported over the years to the author in her work as an educational psychologist). It is divided into the most common problems for children between the ages of five and seven and also those for children between seven and eleven. Of course there will be much overlap – and neither is the list exhaustive. However, you should find enough general information to start you off. With a little understanding of the causes and effects of behaviour problems, you can begin to make your own hypotheses as to what is causing a child to behave in a certain way, leading to selecting an appropriate method of assessment and intervention.

The descriptions in each section use actual words that teachers have used to the author. Later, you will consider how important it is to clarify your language so that the words used to describe

behaviour become clear and unambiguous and not cloudy or subjective. You will see time and time again that each behaviour can have many different causes and how important it becomes to observe and assess that behaviour to see *why* it is happening (Chapter 2) before planning interventions for *what* to do (Chapter 3). You will meet all of these behaviours again in the next chapter where there are suggestions for assessing each type of problem. You will also find that the activity pages have been designed with some of these behaviour problems specifically in mind.

Common problems for children aged five to seven

Anti-social behaviour

These children often end up having frequent arguments or fights and resorting to physical ways of asserting their feelings or wishes (pushing, poking, scratching, biting or name calling). Other children seem to be very angry inside and this means that aggressive behaviour is never far from the surface. They overreact in social situations and end up saying or doing hurtful things to others.

Attention difficulties

These children may be 'always on the go' and tend to 'do' before they 'think'. Young children are still at the stage of learning how to direct and hold their attention, and some may be more immature than others in this respect. Others still have very poor looking or listening skills which means that they fail to respond to your directions for long, even if they seem willing enough to co-operate when given one-to-one attention. You might have found yourself having to give individual instructions as well as group instructions and having to tell a child something over and over again. These children end up needing a lot of your attention, even though they do not set out to attract it.

Attention-seeking

These children are behaving in the way they are in order to grab your attention. You will usually see the child establish eye contact or check briefly that there is an audience before doing something silly. Sometimes these are children who love the limelight or gain great pleasure in playing the 'class clown'. Others seem to *need* your attention almost as a cry for help – your reaction to their silliness is one of the predictables in their lives and the way you contain their behaviour is, in a paradoxical way, a security for them.

Isolated behaviour

These children do not draw attention to themselves at all. They may be difficult to spot at first, but you may notice one child usually playing alone, who rarely comes to you for support and is mostly silent when with others. Sometimes the child genuinely enjoys being alone – perhaps this is an only child or a child whose parents or carers are also shy. Other children seem to be too anxious and inhibited to join in. Sometimes they add to their isolation by electing to speak only in certain situations or at home ('selective mutism').

Lack of compliance

Sometimes you feel that to make a request or demand to a child 'acts as a red rag to a bull'. These are the children who almost go out of their way *not* to do what you ask! If you end up having to say no to them, you can almost predict that trouble will follow. They seem to coast from confrontation to confrontation and to be their own worst enemies. They make you feel that, if only they could learn to comply, they would get so much more fun out of their school day. The problem is that they do not know this yet – they are finding it quite exciting to stay in control. Sometimes these are very bright children or have very determined temperaments.

Over-boisterous behaviour

Some children mean well but quickly become boisterous and over the top. They may behave appropriately in a structured lesson but, as soon as there is any physical activity, they have an adrenaline rush. You might have found yourself being very wary of high winds and rainy playtimes when their behaviour is definitely worse. They find it hard to be gentle, and even friendly behaviour can be clumsily controlled and excitable.

Poor social skills

Some young children seem to lack the social skills to get on with others even if they want to. They seem to end up 'doing the wrong things' so that they find it hard to make and keep friends. Sometimes this is frustrating for them, yet they lack the skills to negotiate and compromise. Sometimes this leads to socially clumsy or even aggressive behaviour with frequent upsets and fallings out. Often there is a great deal of tale telling as a child appeals to *you* to do the sorting out. Sometimes they become overexcited in social situations because they are not sure how to handle them. Often they cannot take turns or share.

Reluctance to 'get on'

Some children do not get on with their learning tasks because they have poor concentration. They daydream, distract others or are distracted themselves. Others seem to go out of their way to avoid anything which smacks of work. This is usually linked either to lack of compliance generally or to a lack of motivation in which it is more interesting to avoid a situation rather than to apply themselves to it. Others too might lack the confidence or the ability to have a go.

Swearing

You will often have the clear impression that the child knows exactly what is being said and also that it is not acceptable. However, when these adult words are being said by young children, it is because of the power they have on the adult world. They provoke an extreme reaction and are a way for children to express themselves and to draw attention when other ways have failed. They trigger blame responses from adults ('He certainly didn't learn that at home.') and are clearly useful tools from the point of view of some children.

Tantrums

Young children have intense emotional reactions and still lack the words to express what they are feeling. At the early stages of developing emotional literacy, temper tantrums are common and a normal part of development. As the child grows older, these can usually be avoided through the use of verbal explanations and consistent handling. Sometimes they become part of an older child's repertoire of behaviour because they have proved useful or because the child lacks emotional literacy skills.

Tearful behaviour

Some young children find it very hard to separate from their parents and carers (and vice versa). They may have found it hard to settle into school and continue to be easily thrown whenever there is something new happening or a supply teacher in. You might have found yourself with a 'little shadow' as the child follows you around. This is a normal way in which these children attach themselves to a security figure in school as a way of developing greater independence from home.

Telling tales

Some children assume almost a teacher's role and are constantly coming to you with reports about what so-and-so is doing. The immediate response for some people is to see this as a means of getting another child into trouble. However, many young children are very literal in their thinking and are striving to sort out what social rules are all about and they may be simply reporting facts to you.

Testing boundaries

Some young children have not yet learned that 'a rule is a rule' or that 'no means no'. They may be learning this for the first time in your class, and part of learning about behaviour is to test the boundaries. This is the method children use to generalise behaviour rules to different situations. In a similar way, you will find children testing the boundaries when they come into a new class and meet new adults in their lives.

Common problems for children aged seven to eleven
Angry outbursts

For older children, angry outbursts associated with their earlier temper tantrums can remain within their repertoires. These are the children described as having a short fuse, who seem to have no shades of grey when it comes to handling their frustrations. Sometimes you will know what has made them so reactive – perhaps there are issues at the moment that are bound to have made them more tense. For others, the outbursts are a long-term problem – perhaps because they still have much to learn about managing their emotions. Just occasionally children are angry for organic reasons: low blood sugar can cause irritability and some medical conditions and medications can also contribute to this.

Anxious behaviour

Quite often, younger children who had difficulties in separating from parents and carers early on, or who were rather isolated in their play, go on to be anxious when they are older. For others, a particular event (such as a major change in their lives, illness or trauma) can set off an anxiety state. We all show anxious behaviour – it is a normal response to certain events – but some children become so anxious that it gets in the way of their happiness, sociability and learning.

Argumentative behaviour

Some children will argue anything. You may have tried to argue back and found this unproductive. Occasionally this behaviour is done for attention, but more often you will find that you are working with a bright child who genuinely thinks outside the box. Children do not come ready packaged with respect for others and you will have found yourself very busy keeping one step ahead. Occasionally, you will have found yourself simply restating rules ('because that is what we do in this class') and not being drawn into the argument. Other children are very competitive and find themselves in constant rivalry with others with frequent squabbles as if jostling for position.

Attention difficulties

Some children continue to have great difficulties in focusing and maintaining attention despite your interventions and teaching. By the age of seven and above, some of these children may have received a diagnosis of attention deficit/hyperactivity disorder (AD/HD) and some may be on medication. Even so, they need careful monitoring in order to make sure there are no adverse effects from the drug. The children without the element of hyperactivity – those who have attention deficit disorder (ADD) – are more difficult to identify since their poor attention will not be so obvious to you.

Blankness and isolation

Sometimes this is associated with depression or high levels of anxiety. Occasionally, children have genuine blank spells in which their whole consciousness slips for a brief second. These episodes are worth identifying since they can signify a type of *petit mal* epilepsy that can be treated. A child who continues to be extremely shy or lacks social skills can also grow up to be isolated. In small classes and schools, or for children from ethnic minorities, isolation can simply be a product of lack of friendship opportunities or language barriers.

Bullying

There is no stereotype for a bully or a victim, and both of these can be represented in a wide cross-section of children. You will find it safest to identify *bullying behaviour* (rather than *bullies* and *victims*). All schools should now have clear behaviour policies including what they do to prevent and handle bullying. Often bullying is directed towards a child who is different in some way. Both bullies and victims may have low self-esteem.

Destructive behaviour

Some children appear to take a pleasure in destroying property or in vandalism. Quite often this is associated with groups of children egging each other on. For others, it may be linked to worryingly low self-esteem in which the child destroys their own work or successes, almost as if to prove that their efforts are worthless.

Lying

Children can lie to get out of trouble, to divert blame on to others, or even to fabricate a life which seems more attractive or interesting for them. Whereas under-sevens can easily drift into fantasy, most children aged seven and over have a clear idea of fact and fantasy and so lying can become more deliberate and functional for them.

Physical aggression

Children who show high levels of physical aggression have usually grown up in that pattern. They are generally angry children and have often had models of aggressive behaviour from adults around them. Occasionally you see this type of behaviour from physically large children who have learned over time that using their brute strength can acquire results for them. Others really enjoy fighting or have become carried along by the favourite violent cartoon or TV series of the moment.

Poor social skills

Even if a child has mastered the social skills needed to get on in Key Stage 1, they might still find the more complex social rules involved in the daily life of Key Stage 2 more of a challenge. Older children need more complex skills to be able to listen, to support, to negotiate, to see the other point of view, to influence others appropriately and to assert themselves. Poor social skills therefore continue to be a common cause of behaviour difficulties right into adolescence and beyond.

Reluctance to work

You should always suspect learning difficulty as a cause of reluctance to work. If a child cannot experience success in learning, then it becomes easier and safer to procrastinate, to distract, or to avoid work altogether. Lack of motivation and interest can also be a cause, as can anxiety and having 'something always on the mind'. Reluctance to 'get on with it' can also be linked to poor study habits and weak personal organisation skills.

Stealing

In seven-year-olds and above, stealing often has a functional cause – a child steals something because it is wanted. Occasionally, children behave like magpies and gather a hoard of possessions together even though they are not needed or wanted. These children often have some kind of unhappiness or anxiety in their lives and it can be a form of 'comfort stealing'. Again it is helpful if you can see this as *stealing behaviour*, rather than see the children as *thieves*.

ASSESSING CHILDREN WITH BEHAVIOURAL DIFFICULTIES

Some children display behaviour which needs additional and different approaches from usual in order to manage it. These are the children who have 'SEN'.

When does a child have SEN?

While it is clear that certain children in your class are working through the National Curriculum at a slower rate than other children and therefore may have SEN related to their *learning* difficulties, it is not so easy when it comes to *behavioural* difficulties. Remind yourself of the legal definition of SEN so that you can then apply this to your situation. Children have SEN if they have a *learning difficulty* which calls for approaches which are *additional or different* to usual. Learning difficulties can have many different causes, including instances in which a child's behaviour or emotions get in the way of their learning. These difficulties have to be *significantly greater than for other children their age.* In other words, you are expected to be able to include a wide range of behaviour and social maturity within your class as part of your every day differentiation – children's behaviour always comes in many different forms and this does not mean that all these children have SEN. However, there will usually be one or more children in your class whose behaviour difficulties have persisted over time, and are extreme or unusual enough to demand individual approaches and plans. These are the children who have SEN on account of their behavioural and emotional difficulties and require monitoring under the SEN *Code of Practice* (DfES 2001).

What are the legal implications?

Your obligations under the SEN *Code of Practice* are described in the *Special Needs Handbook* by Hannah Mortimer (Scholastic). Supposing that you have found that additional or different approaches are necessary for managing a child's behaviour and helping them to access the curriculum. At this stage, you will discuss the child's needs with parents or carers and decide to place that child's name on your SEN record. Once a child's SEN have been identified, you should intervene through School Action. When reviewing the child's progress and the help they are receiving, the SENCO and teacher might decide to seek alternative approaches to behaviour management through the support of the outside professional services. When you plan interventions working with outside professionals, this is known as taking School Action Plus.

For a very few children, the help provided by School Action Plus will still not be sufficient to ensure satisfactory progress in the child's behaviour, even when it has run over several review periods. The provider, external professional and parents may then decide to ask the LEA to consider carrying out a statutory assessment of the child's SEN perhaps leading to a statement of SEN for the child.

Target setting

One characteristic of School Action is the writing of an individual education plan (IEP). This is a plan which should lead to the child making progress. When planning for a child who has behavioural, emotional and social difficulties, this is sometimes called the 'individual behaviour plan' (IBP). First, you should *formulate* a plan. You can then *implement* your plan over a period of time and *monitor* how effective it is in bringing about change. This evidence allows you to *evaluate* the effectiveness of your interventions. There is a photocopiable form, which you can adapt for your situation, on page 32. This plan should be seen as an integrated aspect of the curriculum planning for the whole class.

Each IBP should contain three or four clear behaviour targets which the child can be expected to achieve with support. It should be reviewed regularly with parents and carers and these reviews will usually be arranged and chaired by the SENCO. You can involve parents or carers more fully in the reviews by using the photocopiable form on page 33. It may help to meet with them to take them through it verbally.

Keeping children central

Children with SEN should become progressively more involved in setting and evaluating targets through their individual education/behaviour plans in order to improve their confidence and self-image. You can involve children in the review by taking time to talk to the child before the review meeting. Find out what the child likes doing best in school, what they find difficult, where more support would be welcomed and whether there are any worries. Sentence completion can be a helpful approach for children to use (for example: 'I don't like it when…' or, 'I like it when…') and you will find a photocopiable sheet to adapt on page 34. It always helps to keep children central to the discussion if there are examples of their work, photographs, observations and even video clips present for everyone to see and, hopefully, celebrate any positive change.

How can I get support?

It is likely in the future that the bulk of the responsibility and funding for managing SEN will pass to schools, unless a child needs a very high level of funded support because of complex and multiple needs. Of course, extra support does not only mean extra staffing and this book describes all the other ways in which you can influence how children's SEN are catered for in your class:

- your expectations of the children and the kinds of demands you place on them
- your teaching styles and approaches
- school policy and practice for managing behaviour
- how you use resources and the layout of the classroom
- the ethos of the school and classroom
- how the children think and feel about themselves
- how closely you can work with home
- how well staff support one another.

What do I do first?

The first step with a behavioural difficulty is to gather information through talking with the family and any other professional involved, and through observing the behaviour itself. Not only does this provide you with useful information but it gives you 'thinking time' to work out what you can do about it. It also helps you to consider what it is the child is actually doing in clear unambiguous terms so that everyone can agree where you start from. Use specific words like 'hit', 'threw' and 'snatched', rather than 'was aggressive', 'was disruptive' and 'was naughty' which could be ambiguous, open to interpretation and also open to dispute. When discussing matters with parents and carers, you can usually find a positive way of embedding this information, for example: 'Jack finds it very hard to share and this is a shame because he is not enjoying friendships as much as he could. That is why he seems to snatch and hit others, so we want to make a plan to teach him to…'

Once a problem has been identified everyone will be looking towards you to 'do something'. When you gather information, you are clearly doing something even though you may not have a plan of action formulated. Sometimes the very act of standing back a little and observing what is going on gives you the emotional distance to think about the problem more objectively. There are various ways in which you can observe and record problem behaviour. When this is done prior to a behavioural intervention it is called collecting 'baseline' information.

Observation and assessment

ABC diary

Keep a diary of any incidents, recording what the child was actually doing when demonstrating that behaviour problem, what seemed to lead up to it and what the consequences were. Write clearly and objectively, describing observable actions and using non-judgemental language. This is called an 'ABC diary' because it records:

A – the antecedent: what led up to the behaviour or what was happening just before it. (For example: 'Jack was working with Tom, recording his measurements with the spring balance').
B – the behaviour itself: exactly what occurred, recorded in clear unambiguous words. (For example: 'Jack snatched the balance off Tom and stretched it out of shape.')
C – the consequences of the behaviour: what happened as a result, including what happened to the child. (For example: 'Tom shouted abuse and Jack tried to hit him.')

ABC behaviour chart

An *ABC behaviour chart* can help to identify any factors that may be affecting the child's behaviour. Like the *ABC diary*, it allows you to gather information about all kinds of behaviour and not to identify the problem behaviour in advance. There is a photocopiable form that you can use in your setting on page 35.

By recording the antecedent (what happened before the behaviour took place), the behaviour (exactly what the child did) and the consequence (what happened as a result of the behaviour), a clearer view of the context of the behaviour can be gained. For every entry of a difficult behaviour, record one occasion when the child was behaving appropriately or especially well. This provides you with information about the situations which work well for the child as well as those which are not so successful. Both of these ABC approaches provide you with information about the *context* of the behaviour and any *patterns* in it.

Attainment levels

When you are working with any entrenched behavioural problem it is worth assessing if the child can actually perform what it is you are expecting them to. Sometimes the use of your usual attainment tests (including SATs) can flag that some children might have a genuine specific learning difficulty or be struggling to succeed in their school work.

Counting behaviours

Sometimes a behaviour is so evident that you can actually count the number of times it happens during a school day. This is only possible if you are clear in your mind what constitutes the problem behaviour and when you will count it as happening. Your own idea of 'being naughty' might be different to other people's definitions, so describe the behaviour in clear, objective ways (for example: 'Michael took George's work and tore it up on two occasions.'). Behaviours which might lend themselves to a frequency count include throwing equipment, upsetting chairs, kicking or climbing on to the tables.

Fly-on-the-wall observation

Try to arrange cover or classroom assistance so that you can observe a child over a continuous period of time (for example: 30 minutes) and write down what the child is doing and how they are interacting in clear, unambiguous terms. Record the time in the left-hand margin so that you will have an idea of how long the child was working in a certain area, with certain other children or demonstrating a certain behaviour. Later, you can look through the observation and identify any patterns to the behaviour.

Interviews

You always need to talk to the child. Spending a short amount of individual time with the child can go a long way towards providing you with clues as to why they are behaving in a particular way. Even if you receive angry silence, this can tell you a great deal. It helps to hold these interviews at a quiet time of the day when you will not be interrupted (and not just as a response to trouble). By doing it in this way the child will see you as a problem-solver as well as the source of discipline.

Interviews with parents and carers are an integral part of individual behaviour planning for children. Find out whether there are similar difficulties at home and what seems to help. Look for family patterns and factors. Look back into the child's development to assess whether the problem is long-standing. Handle these interviews in the spirit of gathering information rather than relaying a list of problems, making it clear that your intention is to work with the family to improve things.

Measuring behaviours

Other behaviours can be measured in terms of their duration – perhaps a child cried for ten minutes one day or played happily for 20 minutes continuously. The whole point of measuring the behaviour in some way is to enable you to see change and monitor the intervention you have planned.

Observational checklists

There are some checklists available to help with assessments of behaviour and often these are put together by a school, for example covering the teaching objectives of your personal, social and health education programme. If a checklist is *standardised* it tells you what particular skills or behaviours are typical of a certain age or stage. Standardised behaviour checklists sometimes need a specialist to analyse them, such as the 'Conner's checklists' for assessing behaviour related to AD/HD. You will find details of suppliers on page 95 and the catalogues themselves provide information about which checklists are available to which type of professional.

Questionnaires

Sometimes you can use a questionnaire directed to the pupil, to colleagues or to parents or carers in order to gather information about a child's behaviour, feelings or levels of self-esteem and confidence. In some cases (perhaps if literacy skills are a problem) you might decide to use the questionnaire as a structured interview, talking the recipient through it rather than handing it out for completion. Schools often design these questionnaires themselves (such as in a whole-school survey on bullying). You will find details of commercial suppliers on page 95 and again the catalogues themselves provide information about which resources are available to which type of professional.

Spot observations

With older children, it is helpful sometimes to use spot observations to see whether a child is 'off task' or 'on task'. These depend on your being able to have a clear definition of what 'being on task' constitutes for that child and that activity. Supposing you were worried about a child whose behaviour is very solitary. Each five minutes you could observe the child briefly and record whether they were working on a co-operative group task on their own or with others and keep a simple tally count. This would again give you a baseline against which you could measure positive change. Perhaps

your baseline observations show that the child was working on their own for ten out of twelve observations. After you have worked on encouraging more co-operative learning, you might be able to record a 'post baseline' of only three out of twelve. You will find a framework for taking five-minute observations on page 36. The whole observation need only take one hour of quick five-minute spot-checks. Repeat it in different situations and on different days so that you are sure you have a meaningful sample.

Choosing the best form of assessment

There is no hard-and-fast rule about how you should assess behavioural, emotional and social difficulties in your class. Make a pragmatic decision based on your particular experience, resources and situation. The main aim is to gather evidence about where you started from, so that you can then gather evidence about the progress (or lack of it) being made. It is the assessment which forms your plan and this allows you to enter the formulate-implement-monitor-evaluate cycle you met on page 22. Without assessment, you have no clear idea about what the problem is, no idea about the context and pattern of the behaviour and therefore no idea about what interventions might work. Without a clear starting point, you have no baseline against which to measure change and improvement.

You will find the same types of behaviour you met in Chapter 1 listed below. Against each are the main ways in which teachers can assess that behaviour in order to plan the kinds of interventions listed in Chapter 3. The activity pages that put these approaches into practice will then make more sense to you. You will be in a better position to use the activities flexibly as 'springboards' to your own ideas, rather than as rigid recipes.

Angry outbursts
● Use an *ABC diary* or *ABC behaviour chart* to look for patterns. Do you think the angry outbursts are a form of out-of-control temper tantrum, an extreme response to criticisms or slights, unprovoked episodes of aggression or acts of frustration? What actually happens? What triggers them? When are they less likely to take place?
● If you suspect frustration linked to the child's work, check the child's *attainment levels* and look for any other learning difficulties.
● *Count* the incidences so that you can monitor change.
● Use *interviews*. Ask families about their child's early development – did their child always have a 'short fuse'?
● Use *questionnaires* for information from the child's point of view.

Anti-social behaviour
● Use an *ABC diary* or *ABC behaviour chart* to look for patterns. What is the child actually doing that is anti-social? What triggers this behaviour? When is it less likely to take place? How do the other children react? Does the child lack social skills (in other words, the child wants to be social but does not know how to be) or are they expressing their feelings in inappropriate ways?

● Use a *fly-on-the-wall observation* to see the behaviour in greater context – you might have missed some subtle triggers that are playing a part in keeping the anti-social behaviour going.
● Use *interviews*. Ask parents about their child's early development – did their child always find friendships difficult?
● Use *observational checklists* if you feel that the child might be behaving in an unusual way because of a developmental difficulty, such as Asperger's Syndrome or AD/HD.

Anxious behaviour
● If you suspect anxiety linked to the child's work, check the child's *attainment levels* and look for any other learning difficulties.
● *Count* the incidences of any observable behaviours (such as tearfulness) so that you can monitor change.
● Use *interviews*. Look for family patterns and factors. Ask parents about early development – was their child always anxious and were there problems in separating?
● Use *questionnaires* for information from the child's point of view.
● Use *spot observations* to gauge the child's level of anxiety in any given situation. How does the child demonstrate anxiety? (that is, what does the child actually do?).

Argumentative behaviour
● Use an *ABC diary* or *ABC behaviour chart* to look for patterns. Who does the child argue with and why?
● Use a *fly-on-the-wall observation* to watch the behaviour in greater context – you might have missed some subtle triggers from other children that are playing a part in provoking the arguments.
● *Interview* the child about incidents to try to understand their point of view. *Interview* parents or carers to see whether the problem is confined to school and ask about the child's behaviour with siblings.
● *Count* the disputes in a typical school day so that you can measure change.

Attention difficulties
● Use an *ABC behaviour chart* to gather information about situations in which attention is poor and situations when the child can concentrate for longer.
● Check *attainment levels* to see how far these are being affected by the child's pattern of attention and concentration. Look especially at the child's language and level of understanding and hearing in case this is why they are not following instructions.
● Use a *fly-on-the-wall observation* to see in more detail what the child is doing when not attending.
● Use *interviews* to obtain a family context.
● *Observational checklists* and *questionnaires* to colleagues or parents can be a useful way of assessing whether or not the child's level of inattention or activity is higher than usual for that age and stage.
● Use *spot observations* to assess if the child is sitting appropriately, 'on task', working appropriately, and so on.

Attention-seeking

● Use an *ABC diary* or *ABC behaviour chart* to look for patterns. What triggers the incidences? When are they less likely to take place? How do the other children react? Does the child seek only positive attention, or are they just as quick to seek a negative response.

● Use a *fly-on-the-wall observation* to watch the behaviour in greater context – you might have missed some subtle triggers from other children that are playing a part in provoking any silliness. Watch especially the child's behaviour just before the incident (are they checking to make sure that there is an audience watching?).

● *Count* the incidences in a typical school day so that you can measure change. Keep a separate tally of positive behaviour leading (appropriately) to positive attention and of negative behaviour which also (inappropriately) draw attention to the child.

Blankness

● Check *attainment levels* to make sure the child understands the work required of them. Check especially their understanding of language and their hearing and listening skills.

● Use *questionnaires* to check levels of self-esteem if a child is quietly not engaging.

● Use *interviews* to check general health at home, any family history of blankness, any family pattern of shyness and to make sure the child is getting enough sleep. *Interview* the child to see if there might be any current worries or anxieties.

● Use *spot observations* to check whether a child is looking blank, then intervene with the child's name and a touch to see if they can be easily roused. This will help you sort out if there might be a neurological difficulty, such as a form of epilepsy.

Bullying

● Use an *ABC behaviour chart* for reported incidents and look for patterns. What is the child actually doing to bully others? Who is it directed towards? How do the other children (including any audience) react?

● Use *interviews* with the child, observers and 'victim'. Try to gather information in the 'no-blame' way (see page 47).

● Use *spot observations* at break times, recording any evidence of threatening behaviour.

● Use *questionnaires* as part of a whole-school approach to gauge the perceived extent and effects of bullying.

Destructive behaviour

● Use an *ABC diary* or *ABC behaviour chart* to look for patterns. What leads up to the behaviour? When is it less likely to take place? How do other people react?

● Use *interviews*. Look for patterns at home and look at how parents view and react to their child's successes and failures.

● Use *questionnaires* and *spot observations* to check the child's feelings and self-esteem – does the underlying emotion seem to be anger, frustration or unhappiness?

Isolated behaviour
● Use *questionnaires* to check self-esteem and friendships.
● Use *interviews* to check family patterns, such as shyness. Ask parents if the child had opportunities to mix when younger or out of school? *Interview* the child to see whether there might be any current worries or anxieties.
● Use *spot observations* to check whether the child is mixing with others and note the context each time. Look for whether the child has developed appropriate social skills for making friends.

Lack of compliance
● Use an *ABC diary* or *ABC behaviour chart* to look for patterns. When does the child refuse reasonable requests? When is the child most biddable?
● Use *interviews*. Look for patterns at home and how parents encourage their child to do important things at home.
● Check *attainment levels* to make sure the child is confident with the standard of work set.
● *Count* positive behaviours (for example, when the child complies to a direct request) so that you can measure change.
● Use *spot observations* to assess whether the child is 'on task' after you have given group directions.

Lying
● Use an *ABC diary* or *ABC behaviour chart* to look for patterns. What leads up to the lying? When is it most likely to happen? How do other people react?
● Use *interviews*. Look for patterns at home and look at how parents view and react to their child's behaviour. Talk to the child and establish whether they can sort fact from fiction.

Over-boisterous behaviour
● Use an *ABC behaviour chart* to gather information about situations in which the boisterous behaviour becomes a significant problem to others or to the child's learning in class. Check whether this is part of a wider attention difficulty (see above).
● Use *spot observations* to see what situations contribute to the boisterous behaviour, such as a lack of opportunity to let off steam because of a rainy playtime, or indeed the fact that the child has already been very active at playtime.
● Use *interviews* to obtain a family context.
● Check *attainment levels* in PE to see whether the boisterousness is linked to a clumsiness or lack of body awareness (not being sure where their body ends and other people's bodies begin).
● Use *spot observations* to measure the proportion of break time spent at an appropriate level of activity (that is, not being over-boisterous).

Physical aggression
● Use an *ABC diary* or *ABC behaviour chart* to look for patterns. What is the child actually doing? What leads up to the behaviour? When is it less likely to take place? How do other people react?

- Use *interviews*. Look for patterns at home and look at how parents view and react to their child's aggression at home. Has anything happened to unsettle the child? Talk about what is going on.
- Check *attainment levels* to make sure the child is not frustrated with the level of work.
- Use *questionnaires* and *spot observations* to check how the child is feeling about themselves. Does the underlying emotion behind all the aggression seem to be anger, frustration or unhappiness?

Poor social skills

- Use a *fly-on-the-wall observation* to see the behaviour in greater context – you might be able to see more precisely what positive social skills the child has developed and which situations the child seems unable to handle still.
- Use *interviews*. Ask parents and carers about early development – did their child always find socialising and friendships difficult?
- Use *observational checklists* if you feel that the child might be behaving in an unusual way because of a developmental difficulty, such as Asperger's Syndrome or AD/HD. Use the school's (or design your own) curriculum checklist to see where the child has reached on your personal, social and health curriculum.
- Use *spot observations* to allow you to see positive social behaviours as well as negative or missing ones.

Reluctance to work

- Use an *ABC diary* or *ABC behaviour chart* to look for patterns. When does the child work best (structured or unstructured situations, with certain adults, in a certain group of other children, on certain subjects and so on)?
- Use *interviews*. Talk to the child about what is going on.
- Check *attainment levels* to make sure the child is confident and capable at the standard of work set.
- *Count* positive behaviours (for example, the amount of written work done) so that you can measure change.
- Use *spot observations* to assess whether the child is 'on task'.
- Design *questionnaires* (such as a 'round robin') and circulate them to colleagues so that you can judge the extent of the problem.

Stealing

- Use an *ABC diary* or *ABC behaviour chart* to look for patterns. What leads up to the stealing? When is it most likely to happen? What happens next?
- Use *interviews*. Consider patterns at home and look at how parents view and react to their child's behaviour. Has anything happened at home or school to unsettle them? Talk to the child and try to establish why the behaviour is happening.

Swearing

- Use *interviews*. Look for patterns at home and consider how parents view and react to their child's behaviour. Talk to the child to assess whether they know which words are acceptable at school.

● Keep an *ABC behaviour chart* of obvious situations in which the child swears and try to look for the underlying feeling at the time – anger, frustration, a wish for attention or aggression.

Tantrums

● Use an *ABC diary* or *ABC behaviour chart* to look for patterns. What actually happens? What triggers them? When are they less likely to take place?

● If you suspect frustration linked to the child's work, check the child's *attainment levels* and look for any other learning difficulties.

● *Count* the incidences so that you can monitor change.

● Use *interviews*. Ask parents or carers about early development – did their child ever learn to control their anger at home? Talk to the child about the situation.

● Use *questionnaires* for information from the child's point of view.

Tearful behaviour

● If you suspect unhappiness linked to the child's work, check the child's *attainment levels* and look for any other learning difficulties.

● Use *interviews*. Look for family patterns and factors. Ask about early development – was the child always tearful or anxious? What seems to help at home?

● Use *questionnaires* for information from the child's point of view.

● Use *spot observations*, an *ABC diary* or *ABC behaviour chart* to see how settled the child appears in any given situation. Identify the worst situations and the best.

Telling tales

● Use an *ABC diary* or *ABC behaviour chart* to look for patterns. What leads up to the tale telling? What has led you to see it as such a significant problem? When is it most likely to happen? How do other people (including teachers) react?

● Use *interviews*. Talk to the child and try to establish why they are doing it so much – are they seeing themselves as responsible in some way for what others are doing and therefore for telling you, are they simply reporting something interesting, are they setting out to get others into trouble, or are they seeking your attention?

Testing boundaries and unco-operative behaviour

● Use an *ABC diary* or *ABC behaviour chart* of incidences which stand out to you, in order to look for patterns. When does the child refuse reasonable requests? When are they most likely to follow rules? How does the child respond to set routines?

● Use *interviews*. Look for patterns at home and how parents get their child to follow rules at home. Is the child used to rules and doing as others ask?

● Check *attainment levels* to make sure the child is not disrupting others in order to avoid work which is too difficult.

● *Count* positive behaviours (that is, when the child complies to a rule), so that you can measure change.

● Use *spot observations* to assess whether the child is following rules.

Individual behaviour plan

Name:	School Action/School Action Plus/ Statement
Behaviour difficulty:	
Action	**Who will do what?**
What new behaviour do we wish to encourage instead?	
What will we do in general to make the new behaviour more likely?	
What will we do whenever the difficult behaviour happens?	
What will we do whenever the new behaviour happens instead?	
Help from parents/carers:	
Three targets for this term:	
How will we measure whether we have achieved these?	
Review meeting with parents/carers:	
Who else to invite:	

Parents' contribution to review meeting

Name of your child:

At home

When does your child behave best at home?

What does your child enjoy most at home?

What are the biggest problems with behaviour at home?

What seems to help?

About school

Is your child happy to come to school?

Are you worried about anything to do with school?

How do you feel about your child's behaviour at school?

Do you feel your child's needs are being met?

Health

How has your child's health been lately?

Is your child receiving any medication or treatment?

Are you worried about your child's health or development?

The future

What good behaviour would you like to see your child learning next?

Are you worried about anything in the future?

What questions would you like to ask at the review?

What changes would you like to see following the review?

Child's contribution to review meeting

My name:	My class:

At school

I like doing:

I don't like doing:

I worry about:

I don't like it when:

I like it when:

I get on with:

I don't get on with:

This would help me behave better:

ABC behaviour chart

Problem behaviour

Time	What led up to it?	Behaviour	What happened next?

Appropriate behaviour

Time	What led up to it?	Behaviour	What happened next?

Five-minute behaviour observation sheet

Child's name:
Date:
Adult observer:
Time started:
What behaviour is being observed?

Make a point of watching the child briefly every five minutes. Add a tick where the behaviour is observed and a cross where it is not. Under 'Activity' give brief details of where the child is playing or with what/whom, for example: 'sand tray with Jon'.

		Activity
5 minutes	☐	
10 minutes	☐	
15 minutes	☐	
20 minutes	☐	
25 minutes	☐	
30 minutes	☐	
35 minutes	☐	
40 minutes	☐	
45 minutes	☐	
50 minutes	☐	
55 minutes	☐	
60 minutes	☐	

What fraction of the time was the child demonstrating the behaviour?   ..../12

PLANNING INTERVENTIONS

In this chapter you will read about various basic approaches that can be adapted to help when managing difficult behaviour in daily teaching situations.

The approaches suggested are all tried and tested, though you will need to select those that fit comfortably, positively and effectively into *your* context. Each approach is given a title which will then appear in the 'Special support' section on each activity page. In this way, you can cross-reference support models to actual approaches and have several ideas up your sleeve depending on the nature of the child's difficulty and your context. The approaches fall broadly into four sections: ways of working with a child's strengths, ways of supporting a child's weaknesses, ways of making the most of certain opportunities that arise, and ways of meeting certain challenges.

Working with strengths

Chaining

Sometimes you can break a complex social skill down and teach it to the child step by step, eventually stringing the skills together. This is called 'chaining', because it is similar to making each link in a chain and then chaining all the links together. For example, you might teach an inattentive pupil to ask for help when stuck, by targeting and praising this behaviour. You might then teach the child to work independently at a task for five minutes. Then the child could learn to finish one task and move on to another. Eventually you can string these skills together by setting more complex targets, thereby encouraging that child to work independently.

Face-savers

Usually you will find it helpful to make sure that 'there is something in it for the child' when you are expecting a change in behaviour. You can use subtle ways of turning the situation around to make it look as if the child has made a choice in behaving better, for example: 'Thank you for helping', or telling the other children to, 'Watch Joseph and you'll see how to do it'. You can also give the child space in which to make that choice, for example: 'In your own time, Feras' (turning away).

Good role models

You will have worked out that certain children need to work alongside positive role models if they are to learn and behave at their best. Often this will mean putting children in different groups for different types of activity in order to get the best out of everyone. Make sure you provide more attention to the children behaving well than to the pupils who misbehave, so that the whole expectation of the class moves towards appropriate behaviour.

Hand signals

Sometimes teachers worry that they are singling out a child if they use special approaches to manage SEN linked to difficult behaviour. The fact is that the child is already singled out since you have found that additional and different approaches are indeed necessary. However, the use of pre-agreed hand signals can be a discreet way of keeping a child 'on task'. You might have found yourself constantly asking one child to listen to group instructions. Cue that child in ahead of the instruction by using a pre-agreed sign – perhaps a shoulder touch – and praise the child (or use stickers) at first for each time the signal brought the desired attention.

Indirect statements

Sometimes you can feel that your constant requests for better behaviour have begun to seem like a constant nag and that the children have stopped listening. For older children, the use of indirect statements can make a subtle change to how your requests are received. The statements usually start with 'I...'. This might mean saying, for example: 'I cannot hear if you make a noise. Please talk more quietly' rather than, 'Be quiet!' or, 'We cannot go out to play until these are picked up' rather than, 'Pick these up right now'.

Mediation

Squabbles and arguments can soon build into feuds and long-term disputes and you might find yourself dealing with situations that almost feel like gang warfare and extend into the wider community. Tackle only what is possible within your situation. You can use mediation to use a problem-solving approach to bringing two children together. First talk to one child and listen to that child's version of events. Then talk with the other. Then work out a compromise and agree this with each child separately, seeking their own ideas and contributions too. Then bring the two children together, agree the way forward and follow up a few days later. This does not usually take too long and can save you hours of having to deal with recurring situations.

Motivators

Children are more likely to behave if they are motivated in their work. There are three main ways of motivating children:
- Make the work itself intrinsically motivating – appeal to any appropriate areas of interests (dinosaurs, sport and so on) when selecting topics, themes and tasks. Sometimes children need individually set work at first in order to work with their areas of interest and 'get them going'.
- Make it more motivating to behave appropriately by selectively targeting and praising positive behaviour. In order to do this, you need to tune yourself into noticing when children with behavioural difficulties behave even 'normally', let alone especially well.
- You can add extra motivators which can be used as tokens for good behaviour – stickers, smiley-face stamps, taking the class hamster home, doing a special job of responsibility and so on.

Nurture groups

Nurture groups have been shown to reduce the number of children excluded from schools on account of their behaviour. The groups operate in separate classrooms and attempt to replicate a form of 'family life' based on intense personal interest and positive support from the teacher or classroom assistant. Each child is helped to feel special and valued. There are shared meals and an emphasis on early sensory play and familiarity (see page 95 for reference).

Nurture corners

Even if you do not have a nurture group in your school there are things you might be able to learn or adapt from them. It may be possible to design and set up a nurture corner complete with soft surfaces, gentle music, picture books, sensory play, soft lighting and an available adult ready to offer positive and unconditional time. Use this for anxious, overloaded or unsettled children to withdraw to *before* problems start to arise from their behaviour.

Personal best

Some children may feel that they can never compare to others and success might feel a long way off for them, or even impossible. Expect their personal best, rather than a total improvement, and you will avoid disappointment. Help children with behavioural difficulties set their own personal best targets and monitor how they feel they are doing.

Positive expectations

Some children behave totally differently in different classrooms because the expectations on them are different. If you expect a child to fail ('I knew it would be you causing the argument') rather than to succeed ('In this class we do it this way. Look – I'll help you'), then that is what you are likely to experience.

Positive feedback

Children with long-standing behavioural problems have often learned to 'switch off' from feedback because it is usually negative. Target your positive feedback directly to the child and make it specific: 'I noticed the way you shared the pens on your table, well done!' or, 'I can see you've really thought about this story.' You can also use the photocopiable sheet 'How am I doing?' on page 48 to provide more regular feedback.

Rules-praise-ignore

This is helpful for children who seem as if they are behaving in a certain way in order to 'wind you up'. You can build on the fact that they enjoy your attention, but do so in a way that discourages inappropriate behaviour. If you see a child behaving in an inappropriate way, state the rule (for example: 'Please put that down'), then ignore their behaviour if it is safe to do so, and give them praise and attention as soon as they conform.

Self-monitoring

Some children are slow to develop self-control and behave in an inappropriate way until someone from outside steps in to stop them. Focus their attentions on to what it is they are doing that is inappropriate and then think together of ways to make that behaviour less likely to happen. You can then help a child monitor their own behaviour, meeting regularly with the child to evaluate progress. There is a photocopiable sheet on page 48 which can be used for self-monitoring (where the children issue points to themselves, sharing the points with you and telling you how they felt they did) or for teacher feedback (where the teacher gives the points and explains them to the child).

Shaping

When you are moving towards a particularly desirable behaviour for a child (such as being able to share), you cannot expect to get there straight away. Start by accepting even a tiny approximation to that desired behaviour (for example, letting another child have the glitter stick for a brief moment) and praising it. This is called 'shaping' and many behaviours and learning targets lend themselves well to this kind of approach.

Special responsibilities

Many children with emotional and behavioural difficulties rise beautifully to responsibilities. These give the child very appropriate prestige in front of the other children. Sometimes you might be tempted to feel that these are the children who 'don't deserve' the responsibility and it is not fair on the others. Try instead to find special jobs for everyone who would benefit and rotate them.

Targeted praise

Another approach for managing behaviour is to decide with the child what appropriate behaviour you are going to look out for and praise, such as coming quietly to the mat and sitting down at group time. Sometimes you can use a hand signal or a reminder to focus the child on to that behaviour. Then make sure you do not miss the appropriate behaviour when it happens, praising it in a specific way (for example: 'Thank you for sitting down quietly, Jason'). Recognise that praise has got to be specific and truly meant – if you use blanket praise, children soon realise that their efforts have not been fully noticed or really valued.

Visual timetables

Some children are very strong visual learners but find it hard to focus on to what you are saying. These are the children who often benefit from having a clear visual timetable of what is happening and when during the school day, so that they can settle into the routine. You can use digital photographs of the children at work and play to make this. Visual timetables can dramatically improve the calmness and behaviour of children who are anxious, children with autistic spectrum difficulties or children with rather chaotic attention spans.

Working with weaknesses

Anger management

Some children genuinely have a very quick temper – anger seems to be very close to the surface and they cannot control their outbursts. If you can help the child to *see* that their anger is a problem by *externalising* it (see below), then you can bring them on board in trying to manage it. The trick is to talk with the child and help them to see their anger like a firework. For each explosion, there is a match and a fuse. If they can recognise what lights the fuse and put the fuse out before it explodes, then they have won control. This involves your working together to identify what factors trigger the child's anger (and how to avoid them) and also teaching them strategies of walking away or deep breathing to put out the smouldering fuse. You can use a similar approach for helping a child to manage anxiety and stress.

Assertiveness training

There are certain situations where it would be very appropriate for a child to be assertive – perhaps if another child is leading them on into trouble or when they are being verbally bullied. Assertiveness means replying with a clear statement of what you feel and what you want to happen, usually starting with an 'I…' statement, for example: 'I feel unhappy when you keep taking my rubber' or, 'I don't like you calling me that and I want you to stop'. Help certain children practise using these statements as you review together or role-play certain situations. The idea is that you should teach an emotionally reactive child to make an assertive statement and then walk away from the situation, possibly seeking help from a supportive adult or friend afterwards.

Avoiding situations

When you implement an *ABC diary* or *ABC behaviour chart* (Chapter 2), it may become obvious to you that you could alleviate a behaviour problem significantly by avoiding certain situations. For example, you could arrange for the child to miss assembly for a while, give the child a responsibility to do during break time or place the child with a different peer group. Do not feel defeated by these avoidance strategies as they could be a sensible way of 'breaking the cycle' of the difficult behaviour and working on it step by step as part of a wider plan.

Clear rules

Again, your *ABC diary* or *ABC behaviour chart* might suggest to you that a child has no clear idea of what constitutes appropriate behaviour or that 'a rule is a rule'. Talk together about the rules and then refer to them continually, using the rule-praise-ignore approach, positive feedback and targeted praise. Involve the children themselves in deciding on the class rules, keep them simple and unambiguous and show children what to do as well as telling them. Children are more likely to stick to the rules if they have set them together.

Deep breaths

Anxious, excited, angry or nervous children can be taught a simple relaxation approach. Ask them to sit somewhere quiet and encourage them to look in your eyes and breathe at the same rate as you, as you take long steady breaths in and out. Match your breathing to theirs at first and then gradually slow it down. Make your out-breaths slightly longer than your in-breaths and let your whole body relax with the out-breaths. In time, children can learn to do this on their own.

Developing scripts

Some children are at a loss as to what to say in certain situations and may end up disrupting them instead. Use your observations to identify particular circumstances and help the child rehearse what to say in these cases (for example, how to ask another child to lend something, how to ask someone to play with them, what to say at the staffroom door).

Key workers

Appoint a key worker who can act as a secure base for any vulnerable child, supporting their learning and behaviour and keeping a watchful eye on their emotional needs. This might be yourself, a learning support assistant, or some other adult within school that the child relates to well.

Incompatible behaviours

Sometimes you can encourage children to carry out an appropriate behaviour that is opposite to an inappropriate behaviour, so that when they are doing the one they cannot possibly be doing the other. For example, a fidgety child cannot be flicking pencils if they are manipulating a set of worry beads. The child who rocks on a chair at listening time cannot do so when sitting on a beanbag. The child who is showing everyone else how to replace the musical instruments gently cannot be throwing them carelessly into the rack.

Metaphors

This is another way of externalising a behaviour and making it easier for a child to see that something can be done *by them* about their behaviour. A child who is very tense can be told the story of the balloon. When the balloon is full of air, it quickly loses control if you let go of it and it flies around the room. If you can let a little air out, then you can keep control of the balloon. In the same way, *deep breaths* can release your pressure and keep you in control of yourself.

Positive affirmations

A whole class can do this. Rehearsing positive affirmations together, for example: 'I can do this' or, 'I am good at reading' can actually help to fulfil the prophecy. Practise saying to a mirror in the morning: 'I *can* manage the difficult behaviour in my class!'

Self-esteem building

There are certain approaches that you can use in order to promote high self-esteem and confidence in all the children. Plan circle-time activities, appoint a key worker for vulnerable children, work in smaller groups to help a child feel less socially 'overloaded' and more secure, plan learning activities which allow you to talk about feelings and about behaviour with them, and offer children choices in their learning and activities whenever appropriate. Use positive behavioural approaches, praise and encouragement to prompt more appropriate behaviour.

Separate the 'pack'

Certain playground behaviour becomes ten times worse when the children are playing in a 'pack' – this is a primitive form of behaviour and predictable in schools. Separating certain 'packs' or rearranging the mix of children in an activity can alter their behaviour significantly, as can planning quieter playground areas and teaching playground games.

Social skills training

You will have met certain children who you feel are behaving inappropriately because they lack the social skills to do otherwise. The whole means of managing their behaviour has to focus on showing and telling them what to do rather than what not to. Good role models work well, but you will need to help the child practise the skills as well as watching others.

Take two

Sometimes it can work well to give children a second chance. If a situation has gone badly wrong as a result of a child's behaviour, try making your own clapperboard for 'take two' and then rerun the scene again.

Traffic lights

This is a helpful approach for keeping the lid on a whole classroom. Have a set of traffic lights (invent you own system) and flash up amber as a warning to quieten down and red as a signal to stop. When everyone has quietened down, you can redirect them. Some teachers call out 'Amber!' instead. Another use of this approach is when older children are given red, amber and green cards and display them as you teach, to let you know if you are going too fast for them to follow.

Transfer objects

Some children have a genuine difficulty in moving from one area to another – for example, coming from home into school or entering the large assembly hall. By giving them a transfer object (such as something to show a parent or teacher, or a cushion to sit on in assembly), you can calm these moments down for them. Giving children a definite job to do in a new situation helps in a similar way (such as a message or a package to give the new supply teacher).

Using the right language

Language needs to be clear and positive. You can also use it in subtle ways to encourage better behaviour by avoiding criticism and sarcasm and including statements like: 'How can I help you?', 'What should you be doing now?', 'I'll give you a moment to think about this', 'No one is allowed to bite and I won't let anyone bite you either' and 'Let's start again'.

Visualisation

Tense children can be helped to visualise a calm and peaceful place as a means of calming themselves. Children with difficult behaviour can be helped to visualise an incident again, this time with them behaving more appropriately. You need a short period of one-to-one attention in a quiet place to use this approach effectively.

Working with opportunities
Buddy systems

Pair older children who are good role models with younger children for break times and certain activities, especially where the younger children are emotionally vulnerable, lack social skills or are new starters. Older children who have worked hard to improve their own behaviour can also benefit from the prestige of guiding the younger ones, where you feel this would be appropriate. Some schools have playground buddies who wear special badges and make sure that each child has someone to talk to and is happy.

Circle of friends

This is a special kind of circle time directed at a child who finds it hard to make friends. You will find a helpful reference on page 95.

Circle time

The process of circle time involves key skills required of any individual belonging to a social group: awareness (knowing who I am), mastery (knowing what I can do) and social interaction (knowing how I function in the world of others). You can also use circles to deliver the National Curriculum and you will find suggestions of approaches in the activity section of this book.

Consequences approach

This works especially well with older children. Rather than nag, you turn your words around so that the child is encouraged to think of the consequence of the behaviour rather than the confrontation. For example: 'If you continue to take Jonathan's coat, then there will not be time for any outside play. If you help, we can all go out quickly', or, 'If you can learn to control your anger, then you will find that the teachers stop telling you off all the time'.

The 'certain look'

We all learn to develop this. Practise a certain look which gives the unambiguous message to all that you mean business.

Distraction

When it comes to difficult behaviour, you will already know when the most troublesome times are for your situation. It might be wet playtimes or when a particular child is in. Plan ahead for difficult times by distracting all the children, or certain of the children, on to something different when they are likely to misbehave. If children are left 'in a vacuum', they will fill it with their behaviour.

Humour

Some children seem to follow a pattern of moving from one confrontation to another. The strategic use of humour can go such a long way to retaining everyone's good will and preventing situations from escalating. Humour can be an effective way to get a message across to certain children, though might not be understood by children with certain autistic difficulties. Avoid sarcasm at all costs and make sure you are laughing with the child and not at the child's expense. There is a simple example below.

> Miss Polly is an imaginary child who can be very useful in younger classes. Some teachers use an actual doll or puppet that sits at the side of the room. When a certain child is behaving in a disruptive way, you can say: 'I do wish Miss Polly would stop flicking paper' (or whatever). This is a gentle way of drawing the child's attention to the inappropriate behaviour without having a confrontation about it. Follow it with praise: 'Oh, Miss Polly – you are working so quietly!'

Peer mentoring

This is similar to a buddy system. Pair older and younger children and arrange for them to meet together so that the older child can help the younger child monitor their own behaviour and progress, sharing helpful advice along the way. Some schools pair children up with learning mentors who are recruited from volunteering parents or other adults who have been specially selected and vetted.

Peer praise

Commending a child who is behaving appropriately, rather than reprimanding the neighbour who is not, can be effective in influencing children's behaviour for the better. For example: 'Well done Dan – that's just what I meant. Has anyone else managed yet?'

Solution-focused counselling

Spend time talking regularly with a troubled or troublesome child using the basic approaches from solution-focused counselling. With this, you can help the child rate where their behaviour or their feelings are now (from one to ten) and what they have done to get so far – in other words, you are focusing on their successes. You can also use the 'miracle question' to help them visualise what success could feel like, for example: 'Imagine someone waves a magic wand in the night and everything is better – what would happen tomorrow at school? What would be the first thing you noticed?'

Spot praise

Spot the good (or even the 'normal') behaviour and reward it. Children who have just started to show some effort with their behaviour soon give up if this is not noticed.

Warnings

Some children find it hard to switch quickly into someone else's agenda. Give a warning before a change in activity (for example: 'It will be break in five minutes so finish off now'). Give a warning before a reprimand also, in order to allow the child to save face and change. By doing this, you are teaching them to handle their own behaviour.

'When' statements

Show your positive expectations by using unambiguous statements such as, 'When you have tidied up, it will be time to go home'. This is clearer and more assertive than statements such as, 'Would you like to tidy up now?'

Working with challenges

ABC behaviour plan

Once you have carried out an *ABC diary* or *ABC behaviour chart* of a difficult behaviour (see page 35), select just one behaviour to work on first. This should be a behaviour that should be fairly easy to change or one that is causing most disruption. Decide on a hypothesis as to what *you* think is keeping that behaviour going. You might be right, you might be wrong, but it will give you the opportunity to devise a plan for intervention which you can then evaluate and redesign if you seem to be on the wrong track. Then draw up a plan to change the A, the B or the C.

This chapter contains many different interventions and perhaps you can apply several at once. You might find it helpful to photocopy or adapt the photocopiable sheet on page 49.

Behaviour contract

Older children respond well to this approach. Sit down together and discuss the problem along these lines: 'We have a problem here. The problems for your teachers are... The problems for your parents are... The problems for you are that you are getting into a lot of unnecessary trouble...' and so on. Then continue in the following vein: 'What do you think is going on here? Which lessons are you working best in? Why? Which are you working less well in? Why? What do *you* think would help you remember how to behave better? How would you like me to support you in this? I need to warn you that if things do not improve, this will happen... On the other hand, if we can see real effort on your behalf, then... (at this point, discuss rewards and incentives). Draw up a contract for change and have it signed by pupil, teacher and parents or carers. You might find it helpful to photocopy or adapt the photocopiable sheet on page 50.

Broken record

Try not to elaborate more and more each time a child does not comply with a direct request. Instead, repeat the same instruction over and over – this is known as the 'broken record' technique.

Choices

Use the consequences approach to advantage by offering the child a choice. For example: 'If you do this, then this (positive) will happen – and if you do that, then this (negative) will happen'. This puts the children more in control of their own behaviour.

Count of three

Gain the child's attention, issue a clear direction, then give a slow count from one to three, as you wait for the child to comply. If they do, praise them. If they do not, help them through the direction.

Externalisation

You can separate a child from the problem behaviour by appealing to the child to change what their body is doing, for example, you can ask a fidgety child to tell their hands to lie still.

'Go ahead'

Sometimes you can be a little paradoxical in your dealings with behaviour. For example, you can license a tearful child to cry by giving them a tear bottle to fill up for Mum – suddenly crying becomes much harder. You can also invite two children to spend a whole minute arguing while you wait for them – suddenly the argument has lost the point.

'No-blame' approach

You will find a reference for this on page 95. Basically, you meet with a child who has been bullied and ask them about their feelings. With permission, you then relay these to a group of children who have been bullying or who were bystanders. You ask each of these to think of a way of helping the situation. You then meet again with all the children concerned to see whether the situation is happier.

Sticker charts

Stickers can be used very effectively with an individual child. Keep the sticker charts in your desk and review them with the child at the end of the lesson. They work best when they are tied in to specific targets and when they are linked in with an incentive at home.

Time out

This is difficult in a busy primary school. The idea is to have a cooling down area away from an audience where a child can calm down to the point that you can then discuss their behaviour and agree a way forward. The purpose is not to 'punish' so much as to 'cool down'. Children should always be supervised and safe and most schools and LEAs will have clear guidelines on the use of this approach which you should follow.

How I am doing?

My name:

My class:

I am trying to improve my behaviour in these ways:

1

2

3

I will have: 3 points if I did really well
2 points if I did quite well
1 point if I tried but didn't manage

If I collect ____ points in a week, this will happen:

	Monday	Tuesday	Wednesday	Thursday	Friday
Morning 1					
Morning 2					
Afternoon 1					
Afternoon 2					

My behaviour plan

Name:

Class:

This is the behaviour I need to learn:

This means I will no longer:

What will help me behave in this way:

What might hinder me:

Other ideas which should help:

This is what we have decided to do:

I will talk about it again with _____ on _____

Signed: _____   _____

      (teacher)   (pupil)

Behaviour contract

Name:	
Class:	
The problem behaviour that needs to change:	

My targets will be:

1

2

3

This is the help I will receive from:

Teachers:

Parents/carers:

If I achieve my target before _____ then this will happen:

If I do not, then this will happen:

Signed:

_____   _____   _____
(pupil)   (teacher)   (parent/carer)

WRITING

Children who have difficulties in behavioural, emotional and social development are often reluctant to perform when it comes to writing and recording. Often, this is linked to a lack of confidence and success in this strand of the curriculum. Certain children, and especially those with low self-esteem, are reluctant to even try until they feel they can succeed, so great is their fear of failure. They often mask a learning difficulty by becoming disruptive, and it can sometimes be difficult to spot that there is a genuine lack of ability or confidence at the root of their reluctance to write. Those with *attention difficulties* need you to differentiate written work so that they can achieve success step by small step.

This strand of the curriculum has been included in the book because of the opportunity it provides for thinking about and expressing feelings. Children who are *anxious, isolated* or who have been *bullied* often find writing and poetry powerful ways of releasing emotions and communicating how they feel to others. One example of this is the *'no-blame' approach.* Sometimes it will be a child's written work that communicates to you just how unsettled or distressed a child is and this might lead to you planning additional or different approaches to support them.

Even with written activities, a playfully challenging and therefore motivating approach is helpful for those who are *reluctant to 'get on', testing boundaries, unco-operative* or *attention-seeking.* There needs to be 'something in it for the child' to want to write, and this can often be to use the child's own interests as a starting point. The use of IT can add to this motivation and sometimes offers children with behavioural difficulties a window for public success. You can also select writing topics which cover issues related to personal, social and health education, such as *swearing, bullying, telling tales, physical aggression, destructive behaviour, lying, stealing,* respect for themselves and respect for others.

The most successful lessons will be carefully planned, allow written tasks to be broken down into simpler steps, and have a balance in learning styles, including a certain amount of looking, listening, imagining and doing, as well as writing and recording.

Planning writing activities successfully might involve thinking about how you use your spaces. Certain combinations of children will provide *good role models* for those *reluctant to get on.* Reorganising the seating arrangement can also work well, especially for older children: group tables for co-operation, circles for sharing, speaking and listening, and individual desks for concentrating and writing. You might be able to set up a workstation at a distraction-free side table. This can be an 'office', and can be offered as a *choice* before the children distract others, rather than as a punishment.

In this section, you will find several ideas that make use of these kinds of approaches to serve as a starting point for planning a wider range of writing activities for children who have difficulties in behavioural, emotional and social development.

AGE RANGE
Five to seven.

GROUP SIZE
Whole group.

LEARNING OBJECTIVE FOR ALL THE CHILDREN
● To write a letter of invitation.

INDIVIDUAL BEHAVIOUR TARGET
● To concentrate on a written activity for ten minutes.

Puppet invitations

Children in Key Stage 1 need to feel successful when writing and recording if they are going to be motivated to write later on. Here are some ideas for making written work attractive and successful for them.

What you need
Favourite class puppet or toy; a sheet of coloured A4 paper and an envelope for each child; writing materials.

Preparation
Prepare a letter to the children from a favourite puppet describing how it does not like being left in the classroom by itself at night.

What to do
Read the letter with the group, encouraging the children to show empathy towards the puppet's feelings. Discuss some reasons why the puppet might not like to be left alone in the classroom. Suggest that one of the children could take the puppet home to spend the night at their house. Ask the children to talk in pairs about their homes and families and say why they think the puppet would enjoy spending the evening in their home (for example, what they would have for tea and what games they would play).

Explain that it would be very hard for you to choose who should take the puppet home with them, so you are going to let the puppet decide. Suggest that everyone writes a letter inviting the puppet to come and stay overnight at their house. Reassure less able writers that the puppet can read any writing as long as the writer has tried their best. Allow the children as much time as they need to write their letters. Deliver the finished letters to the puppet.

Prepare a reply from the puppet, thanking all the children for their invitations and stating whose house he would like to go and stay at. Allow that child to take the puppet home that night with others having a turn on subsequent days. Hopefully this activity will successfully motivate even the most reluctant writers to have a go!

Special support
You will find even very reluctant writers will be motivated to write a letter or card if they know they are going to receive a reply. Encourage *positive affirmations* ('I can do my best!'), go for *personal best* and use *self-esteem building*. Employ the *broken record* technique for reluctant writers combined with much *positive feedback*.

Extension
If you do find the children are motivated to write to the puppet, try to keep the momentum going. For example, you could ask the children to write an entry in the puppet's diary when he stays at their house. Alternatively you could set up an office area with a postbox where children can write letters to the puppet.

AGE RANGE
Five to seven.

GROUP SIZE
Small group.

LEARNING OBJECTIVE FOR ALL THE CHILDREN
● To learn how to form the letter 'O' correctly.

INDIVIDUAL BEHAVIOUR TARGET
● To learn how to form letters correctly.

Drive and write

Children who fiddle, throw, take other children's pencils and are generally disruptive and reluctant to 'get on' can demand a lot of your attention. Here are some ideas for writing tasks that do not involve the usual writing implements!

What you need
A large O-shaped track for each child; sand tray; large sheets of plain paper; ready-mixed paint in assorted colours; shallow printing trays; selection of small plastic toy cars; aprons.

Preparation
Protect a large table with a plastic cover. Move any chairs away from the table so that children have to stand up throughout this task. Put a small amount of paint in each of the trays.

What to do
Begin by showing the children how to form the letter 'O' correctly. Draw an O-shaped track on a piece of paper or a whiteboard. Indicate the correct start point for this letter by drawing an arrow-shaped start flag at the appropriate place on the track. The arrow should point anti-clockwise to act as a reminder of the direction in which this letter is formed. Model how to form an 'O' by tracing your finger once around the track. Ask the children to copy this shape in the air, using a variety of body parts (for example, finger, nose, elbow and toe).

Tell the children to stand in a clear space and imagine they are waiting at the start flag, ready to walk around the track. When you say 'go', encourage the children to walk round in an 'O' shape. Next provide each child in the group with a large piece of paper with an O-shaped track marked on it. Show the children how to push a toy car once around the track starting and finishing correctly. Provide the children with a selection of different wheeled vehicles to push around their track.

Move to the sand tray and practise pushing a car in an 'O' shape, examining the continuous circular tyre tracks. Give the children an opportunity to make O-shaped tracks in the sand. Put on aprons and move to the table, showing the children how to coat the wheels of a car in a small amount of paint. Place the car carefully on to a large sheet of paper and then push it around to make 'O' tracks.

Special support
If any of the children find the last part difficult, mark an 'O' shape lightly with a pencil for them to follow. *Separate the 'pack'* so that you can make use of *good role models*. Use *clear rules* for the practical parts of the activity and then *rules-praise-ignore*.

Extension
Use gel pens to make wrapping paper with colourful 'O' patterns.

AGE RANGE
Seven to nine.

GROUP SIZE
Whole group.

LEARNING OBJECTIVE FOR ALL THE CHILDREN
● To plot events on a timeline.

INDIVIDUAL BEHAVIOUR TARGET
● To write about how they feel.

Timelines

Writing about personal experiences can be a powerful way to help vulnerable children release and communicate feelings. Here is an activity based on personal accounts.

What you need
Large whiteboard and marker pens; writing materials for the children to use.

What to do
Begin the lesson by sharing the overall objective with the children – that they will be plotting important events from their own lives on a timeline. Model this yourself by drawing a line that starts at your birth. Explain to the children that you cannot put thoughts and feelings here as you have no memory of the event. Then put 'Present day' at the far right of the timeline and add a recent event to the timeline, for example, starting your current teaching post. Take the opportunity to explain to the children how you felt during this event (for example, nervous about the unknown, yet excited). Add these thoughts and feelings in note form on the timeline. Then model filling in other details on the timeline and, for each event, try to articulate how you felt and why. It is important that you find positive and negative feelings to add; if you demonstrate honesty the children will be honest too. You may add events that produced a mixture of emotion (for example, the birth of a sibling may have been a very joyful occasion, but may also have produced jealousy).

Give the children a set time (15–20 minutes) to draw their own timeline, adding key events and feelings. Support the children through this activity; some will struggle placing events in the correct places. Encourage the children to write as much as they can about the emotional aspect of each event. Circulate around the room asking targeted children to explain one or two of their events.

When you have finished, some children may wish to share some events from their timeline. A positive way to end this session is to ask the children to select one positive experience from their timeline and to describe it in more detail to a listening partner. The partner could then tell the rest of the class one key feature of their friend's event.

Special support
Never put children on the spot to share what could be very sensitive information. Make use of a *nurture corner* if any child feels the need for *time out*.

Extension
This lesson can be extended or developed by asking the children to take one positive and one negative event from their timeline and to write accounts of the two contrasting events. Teachers can really develop the use of descriptive text to portray the emotions felt by the child.

AGE RANGE
Seven to nine.

GROUP SIZE
Whole group.

LEARNING OBJECTIVE FOR ALL THE CHILDREN
● To write a letter requesting information.

INDIVIDUAL BEHAVIOUR TARGET
● To use writing to achieve an end.

School-trip letters

Children who are poorly motivated and reluctant to work need to learn that writing serves a useful purpose for them.

What you need
Access to ICT facilities; local telephone directories; envelopes; stamps; pens.

What to do
Ask the children to face you rather than the computer monitor for the first part of the lesson. Explain that the purpose of the lesson is to find a place for a school trip. They will be writing to different organisations requesting information regarding school trips (the more flexible you can be here, the more motivated the children will be).

Choose an organisation for yourself and model writing a letter on the board or interactive whiteboard. Remind the children of the format of a letter: address top right and the date underneath. Use a writing frame, dictating the contents of each paragraph, for example: the purpose of the letter in paragraph one, the details of the trip in paragraph two and so on. Make sure in your model letter the children have the information they need: the date of the trip, the year group going, the times involved and so on.

Ask the children to log on and open a word-processing package with which they have had previous experience. Tell the children to decide which organisation they are writing to, perhaps providing examples. It is important to choose organisations that are likely to reply. The use of ICT here will enable you to make any changes necessary as you work with the children, while the children can take pride in creating a pleasing piece of writing.

While the children work, look for good examples that can be read out to the whole class. Ask the children to use either the Internet or telephone directories to locate the addresses they need. To end the lesson, ask all the children to print their letters and save their work before they leave the computer. Ask them to carefully write the addresses on envelopes and stamp them ready to send. Encourage the children to share their ideas for the trip. At a later date, the children could be asked to plan the day out. A letter to parents would be needed, outlining the events and timings of the day.

Special support
When children see a purpose they are motivated to write! Encourage *personal best* and *avoid situations* that are likely to lead to disruption by allowing children who may cause distractions to work separately on a side table.

Extension
Ask the children to think about other purposes for writing letters (for example, a complaint or an invitation). List these purposes – they could provide ideas for future writing projects.

AGE RANGE
Nine to eleven.

GROUP SIZE
Whole group.

LEARNING OBJECTIVE FOR ALL THE CHILDREN
● To write an instructional text.

INDIVIDUAL BEHAVIOUR TARGET
● To write a paragraph of information independently.

Paper aeroplanes

Children with short attention spans have often learned over time that they cannot be successful writers. This activity encourages them to enjoy writing short passages, interspersed with practical activities.

What you need
Writing materials; plain A4 paper.

Preparation
Make a paper aeroplane.

What to do
Put the children in pairs and show them a paper aeroplane. Do not discuss anything with the children, simply ask them to watch as you unfold and refold it. Tell the children that they will be working in silent partnerships. Explain that they will each be writing a set of instructions for their partner to follow. The instructions will describe how to make a paper aeroplane. Provide some key vocabulary on the board. Explain to the children that they will be writing a few instructions at a time and trying out the instructions on their partner. When their partner tests the instructions they will not be able to ask questions, therefore each point must be clear and precise.

Give the children an initial five minutes for writing, then ask the pairs to swap their work and try to follow their partner's instructions so far. Remind the children that they must not speak to each other and if their partner's instructions are unclear they cannot begin. Following this first practical period, give the children one or two minutes to give feedback on the instructions they were asked to follow. Were the instructions clear? What made them unclear? What could be done to improve them?

Give the children their next deadline of another five or ten minutes, and stop them again to silently follow the instructions. Again, the time at the end of this session for feedback will be essential to clarify and improve their instructions. Allow the children another one or two time deadlines, making sure that after each one the writer of the instructions is given feedback. To end the session ask the children to evaluate the success of their partner's instructions by showing the aircraft they made.

Special support
Make use of *good role models* have the children seated in good working partnerships. Avoid situations by having any potentially disruptive children seated where you will be working.

Extension
Ask the children to list features of a good set of instructions, for example: using precise and technical vocabulary. These features can become part of a checklist for future instruction writing.

AGE RANGE
Nine to eleven.

GROUP SIZE
Whole group.

LEARNING OBJECTIVE FOR ALL THE CHILDREN
● To write an account of an imaginary event.

INDIVIDUAL BEHAVIOUR TARGET
● To use writing to express feelings about bullying.

Being bullied?

Children can be unkind and are powerfully influenced by each other. This activity considers bullying and the effect it has on how people feel.

What you need
Copy of *The Angel of Nitshill Road* by Anne Fine (Egmont Books); pens and paper.

What to do
Introduce the children to the book and discuss it briefly. Read the first chapter and focus on the incidents of the three children being bullied. Consider each character in turn and give plenty of scope for careful discussion. How does Barry make each character feel? Begin to take notes on the board, including key words from the text that indicate emotions or feelings. Discuss particular situations in the book, for example: when Barry calls Penny a 'moving mountain', how does she feel? Why does she feel safe inside the classroom? How and why does Barry make Mark lose his temper? Why is it that Marigold does not thank the people who stuck up for her?

Tell the children that they will be writing an imaginary account of a bullying incident based on one of the characters in the book. Remind the children to write in the first person, describing their emotions and thoughts. Choose a character and begin modelling an account for the children, verbalising your thoughts as you write. Give each child a particular character to write about, splitting the class approximately into thirds. Ask the children to discuss their ideas with a partner before they start writing.

Tell the children that they have 20 minutes to write out their scenarios. Encourage them to work independently; they will have the opportunity to share ideas at the end of the session. Give the children regular time prompts and for the last five minutes ask them to read through and edit their work. Encourage the children to check the notes on the board – have they covered all the key areas? To end the session, ask the children to sit in three areas – one for each of the characters. Ask the children to share scenarios with each other. How many children have included similar emotions or feelings? Is there agreement about how Barry treats each of the children and how they feel about him? Try to discuss the issues raised by the scenarios in a more general way – how would the children feel if this happened to them?

Special support
You might feel the need to update the school's anti-bullying policy and consider methods such as the *'no-blame' approach.*

Extension
Continue reading the story to the children. Discuss incidents as they arise in school and relate them to the story.

SPEAKING AND LISTENING

This strand of the curriculum has been included in the book because it is an area in which children who have difficulties in behavioural, emotional and social development are particularly challenged. Those with poor attention need you to plan methods for improving their looking and listening skills, and you will find yourself having to focus those children individually by using their names and establishing eye contact before you engage the whole group in a listening activity. Children who have poor social skills may have difficulty in taking turns in conversations or in sharing the floor with others. Throughout the activity chapters you will find that the words in italic can be cross-referenced back to Chapters 1 and 3, so that they serve as a shorthand for the explanations you met earlier in the book.

You will find *circle-time* activities especially helpful when teaching speaking and listening to children with behavioural difficulties. This approach is useful for including children who have *attention difficulties*, are *isolated* children or have *poor social skills*. A game-like and, therefore, motivating approach is helpful for those who are *reluctant to 'get on'*, who *test the boundaries*, who are *unco-operative* or *attention-seeking*. You can also select topics and activities for speaking and listening that allow you to discuss different aspects of behaviour and the way they affect other people. In this way, you can cover issues related to *swearing, bullying, telling tales, destructive behaviour, lying* and *stealing*.

You can prepare ahead for challenging behaviour by planning and structuring your teaching in more detail and breaking the tasks down into simpler steps. Those lessons that seem to go poorly because of inappropriate behaviour are often too unstructured and lack a balance in learning styles. Many children with poor listening skills need to be shown what to do as well as told. Listening for long periods can lead to unfocused and vulnerable children becoming distracted or distracting others. You may have found that children with *anti-social behaviour, destructive behaviour* or a tendency to be *argumentative* fill any 'vacuum' left by lack of structure with generally disruptive behaviour.

Planning speaking and listening activities, therefore, involves a combination of working with opportunities and meeting challenges as they arise. There is the opportunity to start in a small group (or even one to one) and build up to a larger group. Since speaking and listening are involved in so much of the school day, you can embed teaching targets within your special approaches for these children: for example, *using the right language, metaphors, positive affirmations, clear rules, self-monitoring, developing scripts* and using the *consequences approach*. The language you use can become a vehicle for setting *positive expectations* and providing *positive feedback*. There should be many chances to use *good role models* for appropriate language and *targeted praise* for good listening.

In this section, you will find several activities that make use of these kinds of approaches which you can adapt and develop.

AGE RANGE
Five to seven.

GROUP SIZE
Any.

LEARNING OBJECTIVES FOR ALL THE CHILDREN
● To listen carefully to and remember simple instructions.
● To communicate simple instructions clearly and accurately to a small group of children.

INDIVIDUAL BEHAVIOUR TARGET
● To be motivated enough to work, join in and behave appropriately for a whole activity.

Treasure hunt

Children who are quick to take control and slow to comply with requests can be motivated into co-operation by making the learning task particularly fun and challenging. Here is an idea for making them want to co-operate that gives you the chance to set positive expectations and praise appropriate behaviour.

What you need
Treasure maps; bag of chocolate gold coins; simple pirate costume (for example, necktie, hat, eyepatch, parrot).

Preparation
Prepare a simple treasure map on squared paper and include imaginary features, such as 'Shark's Cove' and 'Palm Tree Island'. Write a list of simple directions to the treasure.

Get into role as a pirate captain by putting on a simple costume and changing your voice.

What to do
As the children enter the classroom greet them in role as a pirate. Tell the class that many years ago you buried some treasure on a faraway island and now you plan to return to find the treasure but you have forgotten where you hid it! All you have is a list of directions that will lead you to it with the children's help.

Ask the children to get into groups of three and give them each a treasure map. Point out and describe some of the exciting locations on the map. Give each group a gold coin to use as a counter and then send them to sit in a space together. Tell the children you are worried that other pirates might be listening and so everyone must listen really carefully and only speak very quietly.

One person from each group should return to you. Whisper the first direction to them, for example: 'Start at the sandy beach and go left three spaces'. These children must then go and relay this instruction to the rest of their group, so that they can move the counter on their treasure map accordingly. Group members then keep taking it in turns to listen to, remember and then pass on an instruction to their group until they reach the place where the treasure is located.

Praise the children for listening well and thank them for their help, let them keep the gold coins.

Special support
Place children with behavioural difficulties with *good role models*, *separate the 'pack'*, and use the *rules-praise-ignore* approach.

Extension
The activity can easily be adapted for different age groups: simply modify the vocabulary you use when giving directions, for example: forward/backwards, left/right or north, south, east and west.

AGE RANGE
Five to seven.

GROUP SIZE
Six or more children.

LEARNING OBJECTIVE FOR ALL THE CHILDREN
● To use appropriate vocabulary when describing details to others.

INDIVIDUAL BEHAVIOUR TARGET
● To share and take turns in a small group.

Lucky dip!

Children who cannot share or take turns have less chance of building friendships. Circle time provides an excellent opportunity for teaching these skills.

What you need
Lucky-dip bag containing pictures of familiar objects; stopwatch or ten-minute sand-timer.

Preparation
Organise the children so that they are sitting in a circle.

What to do
Explain that you are going to play a describing game which will involve *all* the children working together as a team. The team must try to score as many points as they can in ten minutes. Start by teaching the children the 'Lucky-dip Rap:

 'Red, pink, yellow, green, black, blue. Who will have a lucky dip – could it be you?

 Red, pink, yellow, green, black, blue. Who will have a lucky dip... it's going to be YOU!'

Demonstrate how to play the game. Begin by passing the lucky-dip bag around the circle while singing the rap. The child holding the bag at the end of the rap becomes 'the describer'. Tell the describer to take a picture out of the bag without letting anyone else see it. Explain that they must help the other children to guess what is in the picture by describing it to them. The first time you play you will find it easier if you limit the pictures to one category (for example, animals). Talk about the kind of things the describer could say to help the others guess the animal, for example: the size and colour of the animal, the noise it makes and where the animal lives.

Encourage the rest of the children, 'the listeners', to listen carefully to the description and put their hands up as soon as they think they know what it is in the picture. Once someone has correctly guessed the picture, begin the rap again straight away. Discuss and praise good listening and good describing.

As soon as the children get the hang of the game, start the ten-minute timer. Continue to play the game at a fast pace until the ten minutes is up. Count up all the pictures the group guessed correctly to find their score. Keep a record of the score so that the next time you play you can try to beat it!

Special support
Use *shaping* and *personal best* – keep the group size small, use real objects and show them to the child with difficulties first.

Extension
Engage certain children as your scorers or involve them in selecting the contents of the bag.

AGE RANGE
Seven to nine.

GROUP SIZE
Whole group.

LEARNING OBJECTIVE FOR ALL THE CHILDREN
● To retell a story.

INDIVIDUAL BEHAVIOUR TARGET
● To listen and respond appropriately for ten minutes.

Draw a story

Children who find it hard to listen are particularly challenged by having to sit still for a story or long discussion. Here is an idea for extending listening skills by focusing their attention.

What you need
A short story linked to any fiction-based text selected from the Literacy Strategy; paper; drawing materials.

Preparation
Read the story before the lesson and decide where to pause for pictures (see below). Have the children seated in pairs at desks.

What to do
Explain to the children that you are going to tell them a story. They must listen very carefully as they will need to retell the story to their partner. Explain to the children that they have drawing materials because you will pause at several stages in the story and they will need to draw a picture for that section of the tale.

Model this process by trying an example and praise children who have listened well and covered small details from the story in their drawings. Give the children short time prompts in order to encourage them to remain 'on task' (for example: 'You have one drawing minute left!').

Continue to read the next section of the story, using expression in your voice to emphasise key features that the children should remember. Give the children time for their second drawing. At this stage the children should be working independently, so discourage discussion now and suggest they share their ideas at the end. Continue to read the story, stopping after each short 'chunk' so that the children can draw their illustration.

When the story has been told, the children will have a series of images that relate to each stage. Explain to the children that they are now going to retell the story to their partner. Ask the children to work in 'telephone pairs'. The children sit on chairs back-to-back with their partner so that there are no visual clues. The children then use their drawings as a prompt and they explain the entire story to their partner and vice versa. Encourage the children to evaluate their partners' listening skills by picking out key facts from the story.

Special support
Beware, this process can be very noisy! Give the children guidelines about using their classroom voices and ensure that children are spaced out around the room as much as possible. Make use of *good role models* when arranging partners.

Extension
Children could make their own book of the story, adding short paragraphs to each drawing.

AGE RANGE
Seven to nine.

GROUP SIZE
Small groups for the first activity, larger groups for the others.

LEARNING OBJECTIVE FOR ALL THE CHILDREN
● To listen and respond using appropriate reasoning.

INDIVIDUAL BEHAVIOUR TARGET
● To remember and repeat a sentence.

Listening games

Here are four ideas to help children with attention difficulties focus and retain information in their short-term memories.

Sentence builders

Ask the children to sit in a circle. Give them the beginning of the sentence, 'I went to the shop and bought…' In turn each child repeats the preceding purchases and then adds their own to the list. Advise the children that this is easiest if they look at the person who is speaking, remain focused and visualise the person with that item. Now try new sentences, for example: 'My favourite animals are… because…' or, 'During the holidays we…'

Think of a number

Tell the children that you have thought of a number. They need to guess your number using the fewest possible questions. Explain to them that you will only be answering 'yes' or 'no', so they must think carefully about what questions to ask. Begin to take questions, keeping a tally. The children should learn quite quickly that some questions will cancel out more numbers than others, for example: 'Is it an odd number?' Once you have modelled this, the children can play games in table groups.

What's in the bag?

You will need: Enough small bags for one per pair and items to go in the bags.

Organise the children into pairs. Ask one child to secretly choose an item from a given selection to place in the bag. Tell the child to look closely at the shape, colour and detail of their item before it goes into the bag. The second child then has a set number of questions to find out what's in the bag. All questions can only be answered with 'yes' or 'no'. When the child has had their guess, reverse the roles.

Chinese whispers

Ask the children to sit in a large circle. Explain that you will be playing a game where a sentence will be passed around the circle. Tell them that each of them must whisper the sentence just once into their neighbour's ear. The sentence will be repeated out loud by the final player to see if it has remained the same. Begin the game with a sentence yourself. Repeat the game, starting from different points in the circle.

Special support

Use *rules-praise-ignore, positive expectations and smaller groups.*

Extension

The speed at which the words flow can make these games more challenging.

AGE RANGE
Nine to eleven.

GROUP SIZE
Whole group.

LEARNING OBJECTIVES FOR ALL THE CHILDREN
● To empathise with another person, assuming their character.
● To ask questions and gather biographical information on another person.

INDIVIDUAL BEHAVIOUR TARGET
● To work calmly and productively alongside others.

Celebrity interviews

Children with emotional, social or behavioural difficulties can often become disruptive when speaking and listening activities lack structure. Here is an idea for keeping them fully engaged, using their own interests to keep them motivated.

What you need
Clipboards; writing materials; interview sheet.

Preparation
Prepare an interview sheet for the children to fill in as they interview the celebrity including the following questions:
● What is your name?
● What are you famous for?
● Tell me about one important event from the past 12 months.
● Why are you a good role model for children?
● If you could, what one thing would you change about the world?

What to do
Start by talking about celebrities and sharing some illustrations. Ask the children to think of their favourite celebrity. Through this discussion introduce some of the important vocabulary, such as discussing whether your celebrities are 'good' or 'bad role models'.

Ask the children to close their eyes and imagine that they are a celebrity of their choosing. While their eyes are closed tell them about some imaginary scenarios, for example: 'You are shopping for clothes and you've been spotted by the paparazzi. How do you feel?' Explain that they are going to be interviewed by members of the press and that they must try to maintain the character.

Put the children into pairs and provide each pair with an interview sheet and a separate space to work in. Invite one child to be the celebrity and the other the reporter, taking turns. Tell the children how much time they have for the two interviews and remind the interviewer to make clear notes on the interview form so that they can give feedback later. Halfway through the time tell the children to change roles and begin the interviewing process again.

When the interview time is over ask each child to assume the role of interviewer. Ask them to take turns telling the class who they interviewed and one key point which that person made.

Special support
Look out for pairs with a particularly dominant personality and make sure each partner is given equal time in each role. Role-play is one method of encouraging *self-monitoring* and self-control.

Extension
End the lesson by asking for children to volunteer to be 'hot seated' and answer any question from the other children in the room.
Extend this activity into work on biographies or historical characters.

AGE RANGE
Nine to eleven.

GROUP SIZE
Whole class but with adult support for the targeted SEN group.

LEARNING OBJECTIVE FOR ALL THE CHILDREN
● To devise a short role-play based on given characters.

INDIVIDUAL BEHAVIOUR TARGET
● To speak confidently in front of a large group.

Flashbacks and flash forwards

Children who are particularly shy or anxious find it hard to speak out in front of others. Drama and role-play make this easier and offer a chance to think about feelings.

What you need
Several scenario cards as discussion prompts, for example:
● Sam is walking around the playground alone. You can tell she has been crying.
● Daniel and Joshua are playing football. Daniel had just tackled Joshua and knocked him to the ground. Joshua looks angry.
● Sarah and Aisha have been arguing. You can see Sally taking messages between the two of them.

What to do
Explain to the children that all behaviours start from somewhere and end with a consequence. Take the example of a dispute over football. One child tackles another and they fall down. The second child believes the tackle was unfair and they become angry. The two children start arguing and then fighting. Discuss with the children what happened before the fight and how this set the scene. Discuss what the consequences may have been and whether or not they were fair. Explain to the children that there are many other factors which may have influenced this particular event (for example, a row that morning at home may have left the child in a bad mood).
Tell the children that they will be working in small groups to dramatically perform 'Flashbacks' and 'Flash forwards'. They will take a scenario of their choice and investigate what happened before and what the consequence could have been.

Split the children into groups of no more than four and give each group one scenario card to work from. Give the children three minutes for discussion and then ask them to share ideas about what might have happened before or after the scenario.

Support the children as they begin adding movements and dialogue to their 'Flashbacks' and 'Flash forwards' at your signal. Encourage them to polish their performance ready to share. To end the lesson, ask each group to show one 'Flashback' and one 'Flash forward'. Ask the others if they know what the scenario was in the middle. How might things have been different?

Special support
Never force a child to speak out or to perform. It is better to use *shaping*, providing them with an informal, consequence-free setting that allows them to make small steps towards this.

Extension
Groups that work quickly can begin to discuss a second and third scenario, selecting their best work to show at the end of the session. Use camcorders or Dictaphones as a more permanent record.

DESIGN AND TECHNOLOGY

Design and technology can be an area of the curriculum fraught with challenges for the teacher, but it is also an area in which certain children can excel and develop kudos. Children who behave impulsively or are *over-boisterous*, who have *attention difficulties*, who are *physically aggressive* or *unco-operative* may find it hard to learn how to handle and use tools and technology safely and sensibly.

On the other hand, for a child who has experienced little success in school, there are golden opportunities for developing confidence along with useful and rewarding practical skills. It is another curriculum area that can be intrinsically motivating for the child who is *reluctant to 'get on'*. Once again, you will find that the words in italics can be cross-referenced back to Chapters 1 and 3 so that they serve as a shorthand for the explanations you met earlier in the book.

The fact that there is a lot of practical activity in this area of the curriculum makes it possible to use approaches such as *chaining* and *shaping*, teaching *incompatible behaviours* and employing *spot praise* and *peer praise* to encourage more appropriate behaviours or new skills. Activities that are concrete and practical (as many technology activities are) are easy for you to observe and therefore easy to use *targeted praise* following an *ABC behaviour plan* and making it very clear to the children what is required of them. They therefore lend themselves to approaches such as *rules-praise-ignore*, *self-monitoring*, *distraction*, *consequences* and *'when' statements* ('When you have cut out the wheels, your car will be ready to assemble'). By making one behaviour contingent upon another, you can encourage the child to keep going and end up with something workable or pleasurable that they are proud of.

You may need to plan smaller groups or additional classroom support for practical activities that involve potentially dangerous or breakable tools. It is worth planning for extra personnel at the beginning of a new topic or when the children are learning a new skill so that safety can be *targeted and praised* before inappropriate or *attention-seeking* behaviours become a habit. Sometimes it is possible to organise an activity on an 'assembly line' principle so that different children are using different tools and equipment to perform different tasks which nevertheless contribute towards a common goal or product. This allows you some degree of flexibility in planning group sizes and the use of any extra personnel.

In this strand of the curriculum, children are encouraged to think ahead and to evaluate how they could improve their work in the future. This lends itself to the *personal best* approach and can be combined with *positive expectations* and *visualising* success. You will find several ideas in this section that make use of all these kinds of approaches. Try them out as a starting point for organising a wider range of design and technology activities for children who have difficulties in behavioural, emotional and social development.

AGE RANGE
Five to seven.

GROUP SIZE
Small group.

LEARNING OBJECTIVE FOR ALL THE CHILDREN
● To use scissors and hole-punches with care and control.

INDIVIDUAL BEHAVIOUR TARGET
● To handle small tools safely.

In the picture

Children who have behavioural difficulties may not be inclined to use tools safely and carefully. This activity teaches them how to handle a range of tools appropriately, and makes it motivating to do so.

What you need
Large rectangular template and smaller oval template (see photocopiable page 72); thin card; coloured paper; selection of different shaped hole-punches; pinking shears; glue; ribbon; photographs of each of the children.

Preparation
Take a photograph of each child in the group. Cut each photograph into an oval shape a little smaller than the oval template to be used.

What to do
This activity teaches children how to make a simple photograph frame. The completed frame would make a lovely Mother's Day gift or calendar. By giving the task a clear purpose you will motivate the children to take extra care when practising skills and techniques. Depending on the abilities or dynamics of the group, you may wish to break the task down into steps in order to allow for discussion of the safe and appropriate use of each tool as it is introduced.

Model how to draw round the two templates on to thin card and cut out the shapes using a pair of pinking shears. These are an ideal tool for children who have poorly developed cutting skills because mistakes are less noticeable. Show children how to stick the oval piece of card in the centre of the large rectangle.

Demonstrate how to use a single hole-punch safely. Let the children punch a series of holes round the edge of their rectangular frame. Then show them how to weave a piece of ribbon through the holes. Help the children tie the two ends of the ribbon in a bow at the bottom of the frame.

Give the children further practice at using hole-punches. Provide the group with a selection of different shaped hole-punches and a variety of different coloured paper. Show the children how they can punch out different shapes and stick them on to their frame to personalise it. Encourage more able children to arrange the shapes in a repeating pattern or symmetrical design. Finally each child can glue their photograph into the frame they have made.

Special support
Avoid situations by keeping children with behaviour difficulties under closer supervision and support. Use *take two* and the *consequences approach* to encourage *personal best*.

Extension
Encourage individual designs making use of the tools available.

AGE RANGE
Five to seven.

GROUP SIZE
Any.

LEARNING OBJECTIVES FOR ALL THE CHILDREN
● To assemble reclaimed materials to make a wheeled vehicle for a specific purpose.
● To gain some understanding of how wheels and axles work.

INDIVIDUAL BEHAVIOUR TARGET
● To try again if they do not succeed first time.

Chocolate challenge

Children who are prone to throw tantrums or who have low self-esteem may give up easily. This is an activity that encourages persistence.

What you need
Box of fun-size chocolate bars; junk materials; a construction-kit vehicle (for example KNEX); selection of wheels or cotton reels; elastic bands; scissors; hole-punches; pieces of dowel in different lengths; small ramp; glue; tape.

Preparation
Give the children opportunities beforehand to investigate wheels and axles and to make wheeled vehicles using construction toys. Create a steep ramp from junk materials and place the box of chocolate bars at the top of it.

What to do
Show the children the ramp with the fun-size chocolate bars at the top. Outline the 'Chocolate challenge' – to make a wheeled container that is able to transport one of the chocolate bars safely down the ramp. Demonstrate this visually using a vehicle made from a construction kit to illustrate the key design features. Tell the children that if they successfully complete the challenge, the chocolate will be theirs to keep!

Show the children the materials which are available for them to use. Working with the whole group, ask children to suggest how they might use some of the materials to construct a suitable vehicle. In particular, encourage children to consider different methods they could use to join wheels and axles to the body of the vehicle. At this point, you may wish to teach the children a specific method for attaching an axle to a base. Encourage the children to make their vehicles as independently as possible.

Wait until all the children have had sufficient time to complete the task before testing the vehicles. Discuss which vehicles worked really well and highlight good design features. Consider how other they could be modified and improved and let the children keep trying!

Special support
Set up a *face-saver* by arranging for the child with emotional difficulties to work out the task individually first before joining in with the activity in a larger group. Be aware that children with behavioural needs will need regular support and praise throughout the task. Work alongside such children setting them small, achievable targets. Encourage the use of *deep breaths* or time in the *nurture corner* if frustrations become high.

Extension
Design a bridge to support the weight of the chocolate vehicle.

Pop-up cards

Sometimes children with behavioural, emotional or social difficulties have grandiose ideas. Here is an activity that helps them to plan more realistically.

AGE RANGE
Seven to nine.

GROUP SIZE
Whole group.

LEARNING OBJECTIVE FOR ALL THE CHILDREN
● To design and make a pop-up card. (This can be linked in particular to Numeracy: symmetry).

INDIVIDUAL BEHAVIOUR TARGET
● To develop a workable idea and see it through.

What you need
One piece of plain A4 paper per child; scissors; resources to use as decoration.

Preparation
Have a card ready-made (see illustration). Put the instructions on the board highlighting the steps that involve the children making their own choices.

Step 1: take a piece of A4 paper and have it portrait-way around.
Step 2: fold the paper in half horizontally and open it out leaving a crease in the middle.
Step 3: fold in half vertically.
Step 4: with the centre crease on the right (see top illustration), design half of the pop-up part of the design. You are drawing on only one quarter of the A4 sheet.
Step 5: cut out the top and the bottom of the design using only two cuts.
Step 6: open out the piece of paper and refold along the horizontal fold.
Step 7: decorate your card, not forgetting the front!

What to do
Tell the children that they will be making their own pop-up card. Show them the one you have made already. Ask the children to read together the instructions from the board. Then model the making process, describing each detail for the children. The children will need to hear hints and tips throughout this process to ensure success. Ask the children to share their ideas about what their cards can be for and what would work best. Remind the children that their design must be symmetrical.

Put the children in mixed-ability groups and allow them to support each other through the different steps of the design process. Share good work as you find it around the classroom. To end the lesson encourage the children to evaluate the success of their card. Have they achieved what they set out to? How would they alter the design for a card with a different purpose?

Special support
Use *take two* to allow several reruns at the activity if this becomes necessary to ensure success.

Extension
Plan and create a simple pop-up book for younger children to enjoy.

Cut along dotted line

AGE RANGE
Seven to nine.

GROUP SIZE
Whole group.

LEARNING OBJECTIVE FOR ALL THE CHILDREN
● To produce a box using a net. (This can be linked to QCA teaching units Design and technology 3a Packages, and Numeracy for realising 3-D shapes from 2-D images).

INDIVIDUAL BEHAVIOUR TARGET
● To look at their work objectively, improve it and provide constructive criticism to others.

Wish boxes

Children who have low self-esteem usually find it hard to be corrected or even helped. This activity suggests ideas to help children self-monitor their work – making their own evaluations and developing pride in their achievements.

What you need
A variety of nets (different types can be used to facilitate differentiation – cubes and cuboids are the easiest, but prisms make nice wish containers too!); scissors; glue sticks; art materials.

Preparation
Make several of the nets before the lesson (they do not need to be decorated). Have desks set out with all the resources the children will need in the lesson. Pair the children appropriately.

What to do
Ask the children to sit in their pairs on the carpet. Tell them to close their eyes and make a wish. Wishes can be realistic, unrealistic, personal, financial and so on. Ask volunteers to share their wishes. Now show the children the boxes already made from the nets. Explain that the children will make their own decorated wish boxes to contain their wish. Emphasise that, as the box is to contain their wish, the children should make it personal and special.

Show the children the available art materials and ask them to explain to their partner four things they would use to decorate their box. List some of these items on a board. Explain to the children that they will decorate their box before they cut it out and glue the tabs to construct the 3-D box. Model this process.

Ask the children to work in their pairs. Remind them to keep asking each other, 'How does it look?' and to expect constructive suggestions for improvements. The children will soon begin to see alterations they can make before they have even asked their partner. As you circulate, listen out for advice, praise these children to the rest of the class, explaining why you liked what you heard. Give regular time prompts to encourage the children to stay 'on task'.

To end the lesson, ask the children to bring their wish boxes to the carpet. Give the children a minute to look at the different boxes. Ask each child to think of something their partner did well. Talk about how it felt to have feedback from a partner – did it help? Show off boxes that children feel really proud of.

Special support
Look for strong *motivators* to give this activity a real purpose – for example, Christmas gift boxes to take home.

Extension
Next time the children make an item, ask them to evaluate their own work as they progress.

AGE RANGE
Nine to eleven.

GROUP SIZE
Whole class split into groups of four to six children.

LEARNING OBJECTIVE FOR ALL THE CHILDREN
● To follow accurately a recipe for making bread. (This can be linked to Design and technology unit 5b).

INDIVIDUAL BEHAVIOUR TARGET
● To learn and concentrate on a complex practical task.

Making bread

As design and technology becomes more complex, children with attention difficulties find it hard to persist unless you break tasks down for them.

What you need
One set of ingredients per group and one set for yourself:
- 700g strong white bread flour
- oven (pre-heated to 230°C/450° F/gas 8)
- 1 tablespoon salt
- 1 teaspoon sugar
- 425ml hand-hot water
- wooden spoon
- large loaf tin (well buttered)
- mixing bowl
- 1 teaspoon easy-blend dried yeast
- kitchen scales
- sieve
- Cling film

Preparation
This lesson would be best planned to begin before lunch and then continued afterwards, giving the bread time to rise. Ensure all the children wash their hands. List the ingredients and utensils on the board along with instruction prompts.

What to do
Explain that as you demonstrate how to make a loaf of white bread the children will follow the procedure in their group, distributing the tasks so that everyone participates. Share the timescale for the process. Begin weighing and measuring the ingredients, ensuring the children copy you. Tell the children to sieve all the dry ingredients into their bowl and make a well in the middle. Show them how to add the water and begin mixing with a spoon. Complete the mixing process with your hands, showing the children what the finished dough looks like. Demonstrate the kneading process and place the dough back in the bowl. Leave it, covered with Cling film, to rise. When the children come back after the first rising period, ensure hands have been washed. Tell them to knead their dough again and put the mixture into the tin to rise once more.

When the dough has had its second rising or 'proving', the mixture is ready to be baked. Supervise the children as they place their loaf tins in the pre-heated oven. Give each child a way to remember which tin is theirs. After 35–45 minutes or when the bread is golden brown, remove from the oven. Let the loaves cool enough before showing the children how to tap the bread out of the tins. When the bread is completely cooled, allow each group to taste the loaves – do the breads taste different? Why?

Special support
Give *clear rules* for safety, plan extra supervision and use *traffic lights*.

Extension
Ask the children to discuss different breads and bread products.

AGE RANGE
Nine to eleven.

GROUP SIZE
Whole class or smaller groups (depending on class resources).

LEARNING OBJECTIVE FOR ALL THE CHILDREN
● To design and make a patchwork cushion. (This can be linked to QCA teaching units 3a, 3b, 4b, 4c and aspects of 2a and 2c).

INDIVIDUAL BEHAVIOUR TARGET
● To develop methods of calming themselves when angry, tense or anxious.

Comfort cushions

Even older children can be helped to explore and enjoy the sensory properties of materials and this can provide a good opportunity for anxious or angry children to relax.

What you need
Paper or sketchbooks; pencils; squares of white cotton (approximately 15cm x 15cm); fabric pens or crayons; selection of other fabric squares (patterned, plain, textured and so on); access to sewing machines or needles and thread.

Preparation
Have a small piece of patchwork sewn together to demonstrate the concept.

What to do
Ask the children to talk in small friendship groups about what relaxes them. Remind them to consider all their senses: music, places, sights and smells. Take feedback and begin to list these on the board. Explain to the children that they will be designing their own comfort cushion – a patchwork cushion cover which reflects calm and relaxation. Show them an example and explain how it was put together using different fabrics or squares of white cotton decorated with fabric pens. Explain that each square must have meaning. The designs should reflect things they find calm and relaxing, and the choice of fabrics must have reason.

Ask the children to work in their groups to sketch their initial ideas in draft form on paper. Circulate around the classroom giving out the white cotton squares as you see good ideas.

Demonstrate the methods by which the children will sew their cushion together. The best results will be achieved using a sewing machine with additional adult support. Once this has been done as a whole-class demonstration, the children can work in allotted time slots on the sewing machine while the rest of the class work on other independent activities. Allow approximately 30 minutes per child.

Once all of the covers are complete, evaluate the project in friendship groups. Ask if the children are pleased with their work and if it is a true reflection of what relaxes and comforts them.

Special support
The whole project could be made simpler by asking all of the children to complete one large square, about 50cm x 50cm, which can then all be sewn together as a wall hanging. Use the comfort cushion when you make use of a *nurture corner*, *deep breaths* or *anger management*.

Extension
Design and make a huge 'Stay cool' hanging for a wall or corridor, using a combination of the children's squares.

Picture frame templates

ART AND DESIGN

This strand of Art and design has again been included in the book for two reasons. Some children who have emotional difficulties can find an outlet through their artwork and creativity, and it can become an important way in which they express and calm themselves. However, they may never find this out until you present the right opportunities and encouragement for them to feel successful. If you can focus on the process of art and design as well as the product, then these children are less likely to feel failure. It can also be an area of the curriculum in which you have problems in pupils' behaviour because your activities may, by their very nature, be more informal and open-ended. Children who behave impulsively or *boisterously*, who have *attention difficulties*, who are *physically aggressive*, *destructive* or *reluctant to 'get on'* may be particularly challenged. With careful planning, it is another curriculum area that can be intrinsically motivating and stress-free for many children. As usual, you will find that the words in italics can be cross-referenced back to Chapters 1 and 3, so that they serve as a shorthand for the explanations you met earlier in the book.

The fact that there is a lot of thinking ahead and practical activity in this area of the curriculum makes it possible to use approaches such as *self-monitoring, positive affirmations, visualisation, consequences approach* and *choices*. Activities that are concrete and practical (as some art and design activities are) are easy for you to observe and therefore easy to employ *targeted praise* using *ABC behaviour planning* and making it very clear to the children what is required of them. These kinds of activities therefore lend themselves to approaches such as *rules-praise-ignore, spot praise, peer praise, positive feedback, clear rules* and *sticker charts*. It is an area of the curriculum at which some children can shine and this provides opportunities for working on positive *self-esteem building*. It can provide you with helpful assessment information when you observe that a child has strengths in visual learning and this may aid you in planning other curricular areas in a more multi-sensory way for that child. It can also include activities that can be built into approaches for calming and relaxing anxious children as part of stress and *anger management*, or a *nurture group* or *nurture corner*. Art can be used therapeutically with certain children who need to work off intense feelings or experiences and might become one way in which they communicate their feelings to you.

You may need to plan smaller groups or plan activities in shifts, so that only a few children are involved at a time. Set up an art table or easel separate from other children if a child finds their artwork particularly beneficial – this might be one of the few opportunities when a particular child becomes really absorbed in their work. You will find ideas in this section that make use of many of these approaches. Use and adapt them as a starting point for planning a wider range of art and design activities for children who have difficulties in behavioural, emotional and social development.

AGE RANGE
Five to seven.

GROUP SIZE
Small group.

LEARNING OBJECTIVE FOR ALL THE CHILDREN
● To use a simple painting technique to represent the feelings evoked by a piece of music.

INDIVIDUAL BEHAVIOUR TARGET
● To be happy to join in and pleased with their efforts.

Musical prints

Even by Year 1 some children have lost faith in their ability to succeed at anything of value to adults. The very process of using paints and art materials can help kick-start the process of building confidence and self-esteem.

What you need
Ready-mixed paint in assorted colours; shallow pots; spoons; large plastic sheet; aprons; selection of different coloured sheets of paper; a piece of calming classical music (or a livelier piece if you are feeling very brave!) and the means to play it.

Preparation
Cover a large table with the plastic sheet. Put the paint in shallow pots and place the pots in the centre of the table.

What to do
Ask the children to listen to the piece of music you have selected. Encourage individual children to describe how the music makes them feel (for example, sad, scared, happy and so on). Next ask each child to decide which colour paint they think best suits that feeling and to explain why they have chosen that colour. Children who find this expression of feelings difficult could be encouraged to link positive or negative feelings to items or events which they like or dislike. For example: 'I have chosen yellow because the music made me feel happy and I am always happy when the sun is shining.' Allocate each child their own space on the plastic sheet and show them how to use the palm of their hand to spread a spoonful of paint evenly over that small area. Demonstrate how to use fingertips to create different effects in the paint.

Play the music again. Encourage the children to close their eyes and let their fingers move through the paint in response to the feelings evoked by the music. When the music has finished, show the children how to place a sheet of paper carefully over the pattern they have made and smooth the paper down to produce a print.

Discuss and compare the shapes and lines that the group have created in the paint. Look for similarities and differences, for example, are there more curved or straight lines?

Special support
Separate the *pack* and keep the group size small. Encourage *self-monitoring* so that the child evaluates the activity personally. Make use of *'when' statements* and provide regular *positive feedback* on the child's behaviour.

Extension
If this activity works well it could be repeated using a contrasting piece of music. Compare the colour choices and line patterns inspired by the different pieces of music.

AGE RANGE
Five to seven.

GROUP SIZE
Small group.

LEARNING OBJECTIVES FOR ALL THE CHILDREN
● To design and make a clay tile.
● To use a range of tools to create different print effects.

INDIVIDUAL BEHAVIOUR TARGET
● To make a simple plan and see it through.

Clay tiles

Children with attention difficulties will have had few opportunities to see an activity through to its conclusion. Because art and design activities are so practical and intrinsically motivating, their attentions can be held.

What you need
Paper; small squares of paper; trays of black paint; square card templates 10cm x 10cm; self-hardening clay; rolling-pins; plastic knives; small pastry cutters and other objects which can be used to make interesting impressions in the clay.

Preparation
Print a selection of sample tile designs to show the children (see photocopiable page 80).

What to do
Demonstrate how to roll out a small ball of clay to a depth of about 1cm. Cut the clay into a tile shape by placing a square template on to the rolled out clay and cutting round the edge of it with a plastic knife. Model how to use the cutters and other tools to create different impressed patterns and effects on the surface of the clay.

Designing the tile: Provide everyone in the group with a piece of paper and tray of paint. Allow the children time to experiment with the cutters and other tools to see what shapes and effects can be made by printing with them. Encourage the children to look carefully at the patterns and shapes and to describe them using appropriate vocabulary (for example, curved, star, spiral and so on).

Give each child a square piece of paper to represent their clay tile and ask them to print a design. Depending on the age and ability of the children in the group you may wish to show them how to design a symmetrical or repeating pattern. Allow any children who are not satisfied with their first design to have another go.

Making the tile: Give each child a ball of clay and help them prepare a clay tile. Demonstrate how to press the cutter gently into the surface of the clay so that it leaves a clear impression. Ask the children to carefully impress their design on to their clay tile. The beauty of this activity is that any child who makes a mistake can simply roll up their clay and begin again. Display the completed tiles alongside the designs.

Special support
Use *'when' statements* linked to *motivators* to keep the child 'on task'. Try the *broken record* and the *count of three* if behaviour becomes silly, and use *peer praise* to encourage *good role models*.

Extension
Provide a sheet of large squared paper (or use sticky paper mosaic shapes) and invite the children to make designs for a floor.

AGE RANGE
Seven to nine.

GROUP SIZE
Whole group.

LEARNING OBJECTIVE FOR ALL THE CHILDREN
● To observe small details from a larger visual stimulus. (This can be linked in particular to QCA teaching units 3b Investigating pattern and 4a Viewpoints, about dreams).

INDIVIDUAL BEHAVIOUR TARGET
● To remain focused on a visual task and become absorbed in the process.

Through the viewfinder

Children with poor visual attention can be taught to see the purpose of focusing on a task, by engaging them in a fascinating observation, collecting or sketching.

What you need
A visual stimulus per pair of children (for example, for unit 3b examples of Indian printed textiles, Islamic tiles or Asafo work from Ghana, or for unit 4a *Titania and Bottom* by Fuseli, *The Ghost of a Flea* by Blake, *The Reckless Sleeper* by Magritte and *Woman and Bird in the Moonlight* by Miró); viewfinders (made from plastic slide mounts or card frames 3cm to 5cm wide); sketch books or drawing paper; sketching pencils.

Preparation
Children would be best seated in pairs with their visual stimulus between them.

What to do
Introduce the visual stimulus and ask the children to discuss it with a partner. What shapes, colours and patterns can they see? Can they see areas of dark and light? Explain to the children that they are to use the viewfinder to focus their attention on a small aspect of their stimulus. Once they have located a spot, encourage them to put their viewfinder down and look at the finer detail. Are the lines curved or straight? Are there areas of pattern?

Explain to the children that they are going to be sketching the area they have chosen with their viewfinders, using light pencil strokes that can be made darker if necessary. Model this process on a flip chart, talking the children through it. Give them a time limit of no more than ten minutes to capture what is in their viewfinder. Reassure the children that their sketches will not necessarily be aesthetically pleasing and will look abstract.

When the ten minutes is up, ask the children to reposition their viewfinder and repeat the activity. Try to fit three ten-minute sessions into this part of the lesson. To end the session, encourage the children to discuss techniques they found useful. Ask the children to open their sketchbooks on their best effort. Then ask them to walk silently around the classroom looking for good examples of work.

Special support
Encourage children who are struggling to select areas of pattern rather than elaborate detail. Use *targeted praise* and *good role models*.

Extension
More able children could apply this principle with scale and draw a magnified version of what they see in their viewfinder. Less able children could be given the aid of a grid to help them sketch in the correct proportions.

AGE RANGE
Seven to nine.

GROUP SIZE
Small group.

LEARNING OBJECTIVE FOR ALL THE CHILDREN
● To mix paint colours together producing new colours and shades.

INDIVIDUAL BEHAVIOUR TARGET
● To express feelings through paint and talk about these to a teacher.

Paint factory

Children with behavioural, emotional and social difficulties can be helped to use a variety of methods to express their thoughts and feelings and, in time, this can have a positive effect on their behaviour and progress.

What you need
Water-based poster paints in primary colours and white (avoid black); drawing paper; mixing pallets; paintbrushes; spoons (one per colour); pots (for washing brushes).

Preparation
Put up a list of emotions, feelings and thoughts (anger, envy, love, frustration, loneliness and so on) on a board for the children to see. Paint samples of each primary colour to display on the board. All tables should be covered. Each child requires a mixing palette, a brush, a sheet of drawing paper and access to paints via spoons.

What to do
Start by sitting the children together and explaining that we all experience different feelings and emotions. Show them a paper sample of each colour of poster paint. Then show the children the list of emotions and ask if they think any of the feelings match the colours? Which colour would they match with anger or love?

Tell the children that they will be mixing and designing their own colours of paint. The colour of paint they make will be unique – like them! Their paint colour will reflect how they feel in different aspects of their lives. Recap any previous artwork, such as basic colour mixing and how to use the palette.

Ask the children how they feel at school, at home or when they are alone. Explain that each colour they add to their new paint colour must have meaning and reflect how they feel. Send the children to their seats and tell them to close their eyes and think about a colour that reflects how they feel most of the time. Now tell them to add this colour to their palette as their base colour. Next ask them to think about other feelings and emotions that they have at other times and add the corresponding colour to their base colour.

Talk individually to children about the colour choices they have made. To end the lesson, ask children to describe how and why they created their colours using phrases such as, 'I added red because sometimes I feel…'

Special support
There might be opportunities during the individual discussions to talk about *anger management* and to build up *self-esteem*.

Extension
Suggest that the children attempt self-portraits using colours that reflect their emotions, for example, an *angry* self-portrait.

AGE RANGE
Nine to eleven.

GROUP SIZE
Whole group.

LEARNING OBJECTIVE FOR ALL THE CHILDREN
● To produce a flipbook showing movement. (Link to QCA teaching unit Art 6a People in action).

INDIVIDUAL BEHAVIOUR TARGET
● To complete a piece of art based on a topic of personal interest.

Cartoon flipbooks

Even very disruptive and unsettled children can be encouraged to work productively if the topic is of high personal interest and they are given choices.

What you need
Drawing paper; stiff paper or white card; drawing materials; PVA glue; clips of a variety of cartoons and the means to show these to the class; stapler.

Preparation
Make a simple flipbook to show the children.

What to do
All children have a favourite cartoon. Begin the lesson by telling the children that they are to produce their own mini cartoon in a flipbook. Show one you made earlier, so that the children can understand what they are aiming for. Ask the children to share with the class their favourite characters. Discuss the emphasised features that cartoon characters usually have (for example, extra long teeth and ears, big blue hair, a chiselled chin). List these features on the board. Move on to watch some examples of short cartoons and discuss how unrealistic the events are.

Ask the children to organise themselves into pairs and to discuss one or two characters of their own devising and to select an emphasised feature for each. Then ask the children to choose a very short moving sequence that these characters can be involved in. Explain that the shorter this is, the more effective the overall project will be (for example, slipping over, chasing each other in a circle and so on). Ask the children to sketch at least eight images of similar size that show the movements in sequence. Explain that the changes between each frame should be very small.

Once each pair is happy with their drawings, ask them to paste the pictures on to separate pieces of the stiff paper or white card, leaving room on the left-hand side. Line up the pictures on top of each other and bind them into a flipbook, using the stapler. They will need a front cover with the name of the illustrators. End the session by asking the children to evaluate their flipbooks.

Special support
Aim for *personal best*. Encourage children who struggle with drawing and sketching to keep their characters as simple as they can.

Extension
The children could produce images in a variety of 2-D media initially (paint, felts, pastels and so on) and then go on to transfer their skills to 3-D modelling. Small changes in the positioning of a play-dough model can be recorded with a camera and then images put together to build a cartoon.

AGE RANGE
Nine to eleven.

GROUP SIZE
Whole group.

LEARNING OBJECTIVE FOR ALL THE CHILDREN
● To investigate the roles of artists, craftspeople and designers working in different times and different cultures.

INDIVIDUAL BEHAVIOUR TARGET
● To use IT appropriately and to remain focused.

The role of an artist

When a child is disenchanted or unmotivated, it helps to see a purpose to education and to grasp some sense of a successful and interesting future life.

What you need
Access to ICT facilities; art prints that children have used previously.

Preparation
Have a list of relevant websites and a list of artists, designers, sculptors and so on, as well as examples of their work if possible. These could include artists such as Van Gogh, Turner, Picasso, Warhol, Matisse, Manet, Frida Kahlo, Hepworth and so on. Some relevant websites include: www.british-museum.ac.uk, www.nationalgallery.org.uk, www.npg.org.uk, www.tate.org.uk.

What to do
Pair any children who struggle specifically with ICT with a more able child. Tell the children that they will be using the Internet to investigate the roles of artists and craftspeople of their choice. Ask the children to name some artists, sculptors and so on. How do they know these names? Which works of art do they already know? Have a selection of prints that children have already seen and ask the children to identify the artists. Display the names next to the images.

Ask the children to then select an artists and use the Internet to find out as much as they can. They may search the work of Van Gogh (the National Gallery has background), or choose the ancient Egyptians (the British Museum site would be most useful).

Give the children five minutes to find at least one relevant website – any children who have been unsuccessful during this time should probably look at a different artist. Remind the children that they are looking for information relating to the roles and purposes of the artists by asking key questions such as: what were they trying to show, share or comment on? Ask the children to research independently and make sure they understand that their research will contribute towards the end of the session.

To end the lesson, ask each child to contribute the name of the artist or craftsperson and one key fact. Ask the children to consider if they could live as artists or craftspeople when they grow up.

Special support
Break down the tasks into easier steps for children who need more structure and support. Stay close to use *spot praise* and apply a *consequences approach* if needed.

Extension
If the children have the ICT skills, they can open a separate window and type their notes as they search. You could also ask the children to write up their findings to include on an art-and-craft timeline.

Tile patterns

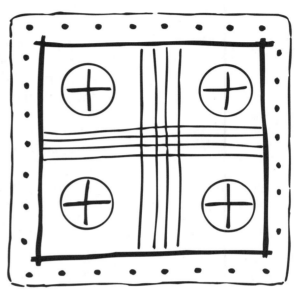

MUSIC

Music can be a real motivator for children and sometimes those who have emotional and behavioural difficulties can shine in this strand of the curriculum. On the other hand, you may have found that you have more behaviour problems than usual in this area, because the work is often less structured, more 'open ended' and less formal. As before, the words in italics can be cross-referenced back to Chapters 1 and 3 so that they serve as a shorthand for the explanations you met earlier in the book.

The children who behave comparatively well in Music are often those who learn kinaesthetically and are motivated by having 'hands on' involvement. These are also the children who have a natural intelligence for all things musical and, therefore, have the potential to succeed very positively in this strand of the curriculum if you can match their learning styles. This involves planning music lessons and activities that have a balance of looking, listening, talking and practical work. Since music can be a strong motivator, it is helpful for including children who show *lack of compliance*, are generally *unco-operative* or who are *reluctant to 'get on'*. It can also hold the attention of those with *attention difficulties* and who devote a lot of

energy into *testing boundaries*. Moreover, the use of *circle-time* approaches (which music lends itself to well) make it helpful for including *isolated* children or those with *poor social skills*.

The lessons which seem to go poorly because of inappropriate behaviour usually lack a balance in learning styles and tend to leave unfocused children with not enough to do, making them more likely to distract others and be distracted. You may have found that children with *anti-social, destructive* or *argumentative behaviour* fill any 'vacuum' left by the informality with generally disruptive behaviour.

Planning musical activities, therefore, involves a combination of working with children's strengths and also planning for their weaknesses. Because all children can usually find some kind of success in music, you have the opportunity to set *positive expectations* and provide *positive feedback*. There should be many chances to make use of *good role models* and *targeted praise* and to employ *shaping* and *personal best* to make success more likely. Music time provides a golden opportunity for using *distraction* and *spot praise*. So long as you make sure the music itself is intrinsically motivating for the children (by using a wide range of styles including popular and ethnic), there will be good opportunities for using the *consequences approach* and *'when' statements* (since the children will be keen to be involved).

In this section, you will find several activities that make use of approaches such as *circle time* and *choices*. Try these lessons out and use them as a starting point for planning a wider range of activities based on your understanding of what works best for children with behavioural and emotional difficulties.

AGE RANGE
Five to seven.

GROUP SIZE
Six to eight children.

LEARNING OBJECTIVES FOR ALL THE CHILDREN
● To understand and respond to the terms 'fast', 'slow' and 'stop'.
● To listen carefully and identify changes in tempo.

INDIVIDUAL BEHAVIOUR TARGET
To join in appropriately with a group activity.

All play!

The use of music circle time has been shown to improve children's behaviour and also to boost the confidence of those who are shy and withdrawn.

What you need
Selection of percussion instruments; teddy; A pair of dice, one with a different colour marked on each side and the other marked 'fast' and 'slow'.

Preparation
Ask the children to sit in a circle. Put a selection of percussion instruments in the centre of the circle.

What to do
Play a steady pulse on one of the percussion instruments. Ask the children to pass the teddy around the circle in time to the beat. Once the group has got a feel for the pulse, start to play at a faster or slower tempo. Tell the children to increase or decrease the speed they pass the teddy around the circle to match the change in the tempo of the music. Tap a steady pulse on your knees. Ask the children to listen carefully to the pulse and then join in. Encourage the children to keep with the beat and stop whenever you stop. Introduce a change in tempo. Invite the children to say whether the beat has got faster or slower. Repeat this activity using other actions (for example, stamping feet, clapping and clicking fingers).

Tell the group you are going to play a game called 'All play'. Choose one child to roll the fast/slow die. Ask the child to choose an instrument and play it in the way shown on the die. Repeat this activity until all the children have chosen an instrument.

Pass the colour die around the circle and let each child decide which colour they would like to be. Now roll the two dice together. The child whose colour is rolled must start to play their instrument at a fast or slow tempo according to what is shown on the second die. Roll the dice again to see which child will join in next. Continue to roll the dice until all the children are playing their instruments together. Call, 'All play' and then signal the children to stop and hold their instruments still. During the game a colour may be rolled more than once. Should this happen, then that child should increase or decrease the speed they play according to what is rolled on the second die.

Special support
Give the child with difficulties the *special responsibility* of rolling the dice. *Separate the 'pack'* by making sure that child sits next to you.

Extension
Invent a simple way of recording the way you are playing on paper to make a simple musical score.

AGE RANGE
Five to seven.

GROUP SIZE
Whole group.

LEARNING OBJECTIVE FOR ALL THE CHILDREN
● To rehearse and perform a simple musical pattern in a small group.

INDIVIDUAL BEHAVIOUR TARGET
● To pay attention and stay 'on task' for the whole lesson.

Animal hullabaloo

Children who find it hard to pay attention are helped by activities that break down into easy steps – for example, a little bit of looking or listening sandwiched between some action. Here is an idea for planning a musical activity that involves all the senses.

What you need
Selection of percussion instruments (with several of each type); six different animal toys or pictures of animals; a screen.

Preparation
Put a selection of different percussion instruments out on six different tables.

What to do
Begin by teaching the children the 'Animal Hullabaloo' song, to the tune of 'The Animals Went in Two by Two':

The animals zoomed into the zoo. Hurrah! Hurrah!
The animals zoomed into the zoo. Hurrah! Hurrah!
The animals zoomed into the zoo. The ____ and the ____ too,
And they all zoomed into the zoo making a hullabaloo!

The third line can be completed using any different combination of animal names. Provide a visual cue for this by pulling two different animals from behind the screen each time the song is performed.

Divide the class into six groups. Give each group an animal name (these will depend on the toys or pictures you are using). Ask them to experiment with the different instruments available to find those that they think make an appropriate sound to represent their animal. Ask each group in turn to stand in front of the class and explain why they have chosen their particular instruments. For example, one group may choose wood-blocks for the clip-clop of a horse, another shakers for the hissing of a snake. Let each child have an instrument of their own and allow each group an opportunity to practise playing their chosen instruments. Bring the groups back together. Insist all instruments are held still. Sing 'Animal Hullabaloo' again. Encourage all the children to pay close attention to the screen, so that each group is ready to play their instruments together whenever their animal is revealed. Everyone should be ready to play their instrument on the word 'hullabaloo'.

Special support
Give *clear rules* (for example, about when to keep instruments silent) and then use *spot praise, targeted praise* and *peer praise.*

Extension
Older children could devise and perform more complex rhythms.

AGE RANGE
Seven to nine.

GROUP SIZE
Whole group.

LEARNING OBJECTIVE FOR ALL THE CHILDREN
● To identify how music can be used descriptively (for example, to represent different animal characters).

INDIVIDUAL BEHAVIOUR TARGET
● To take part in the lesson without becoming angry, anxious or excited.

Carnival of the animals

Children who are over-boisterous, anxious or physically aggressive can actually be calmed by your choice of music.

What you need
Cassette or CD player; *Carnival of the Animals* by Saint-Saëns; large sheets of drawing paper; enough sketching and colouring pencils for all the children.

Preparation
Prepare the sheets of drawing paper (one for each child), by segmenting the page into 14 sections – one for each animal in the music they are going to hear.

What to do
Give each child a sheet of drawing paper and some pencils. Explain to the children that they will be listening to a piece of music and responding to it through drawings. Tell the children that each piece of music represents a different animal. Listen to the first movement from *Carnival of the Animals* and ask the children to consider the possible size of the animal, how it moves, how it behaves and what it may look like. Take suggestions as to what animal it might be. Ask the children to begin to sketch which animal they think is represented. Play the first piece again while the children work. When the music is finished, give the children a few minutes to complete their drawing. Ask some children to share why they drew specific animals – which clues in the music did they hear?

Continue to play each section of *Carnival of the Animals*, giving the children time to draw animals in the segments of their paper. Where the children recognise sections of the music (for example, from television advertisements or films), ask them to think past this as they have little to do with the animal that is being portrayed. After each piece of music, discuss why the children drew particular animals. To end the session, reveal which animal is supposed to be represented by each part of the music. If children were incorrect in their choice of animal, were they correct in their choice of attribute? The movements for 'The Aviary' and 'The Aquarium' are often confused – is this because the animals in question can be small, delicate and glide gracefully?

Special support
Make this activity easier for poor listeners by making it shorter or completing it over more than one session.

Extension
Listen to other pieces of music which represent animals, for example: 'The Dawn Parade' and 'Trust in Me' from *The Jungle Book*. Children could work towards writing their own music to represent animal movement. (See QCA Music Unit 9 Animal Magic).

AGE RANGE
Seven to nine.

GROUP SIZE
Whole group.

LEARNING OBJECTIVES FOR ALL THE CHILDREN
● To distinguish and clap syllables.
● To put a sequence of rhythm patterns together.

INDIVIDUAL BEHAVIOUR TARGET
● To work co-operatively in a small group.

Rhythm patterns

Children who have poor social skills can be helped through circle time to understand how they are perceived by others and how to change their behaviour. This circle activity involves interaction and sharing.

What you need
Selection of coloured card shapes, for example: green square, blue circle, orange oval, purple triangle, red wavy line and yellow star.

What to do
Sit the children in a big circle. Tell the children that they will be listening for rhythm patterns. Begin by clapping the syllables of the children's names in turn around the circle. Make sure the children understand the process of sounding out their name to find the number of syllables and clapping the correct rhythm pattern.

Spread the coloured card shapes out in the middle of the circle. Explain that you are going to clap the syllables of the words that each card represents through their colour and shape – for example, 'green' and 'square'. Demonstrate by clapping the two long beats of 'green square' and ask the children to join in with you. Now change to the two short and one long clap of 'yellow star', again asking the children to join in. Demonstrate clapping two rhythm patterns together, for example, 'green square and red wavy line'. Ask half of the circle to clap 'green square', while the other half clap 'red wavy line'. It is important to encourage both groups to maintain the rhythm or one group may get quicker without your guidance.

Separate the class into groups of seven or eight children and sit them in their own circles. Have the coloured shapes on display so they can be seen around the room. Ask one child in each circle to select a coloured shape and begin clapping. The other children in their circle should join in. Now explain to the children that in their groups they will develop a sequence of rhythms for performance at the end of the lesson. They may choose, for example, to begin all clapping 'yellow star' and then move on to 'purple triangle' and so on. Remind the children that they must think about how many times they will clap each shape (for example, eight lots of 'blue circle'). Give the children ten minutes to compile their rhythm pattern. To end the session, ask the children to sit as an audience and evaluate their performances.

Special support
Circulate around the hall and check that no children are either isolated from their group or dominating it – the emphasis is on collaborative work. Use *spot praise* and *positive feedback*.

Extension
Create a sound script for a story using rhythm patterns. If necessary, teach this activity to a child one-to-one first before the whole class.

AGE RANGE
Nine to eleven.

GROUP SIZE
Whole group.

LEARNING OBJECTIVE FOR ALL THE CHILDREN
● To compose a piece of music.

INDIVIDUAL BEHAVIOUR TARGET
● To work independently on a given task, asking for help when appropriate.

Computer composition

Children who are reluctant to work can be motivated to stay 'on task' if the activity attracts them enough.

What you need
'Compose World Junior' or another similar music composition program; access to ICT facilities with headphones for each computer if possible; projector.

Preparation
Select two examples of a suitable topic from the bank available within the software (for example: Tudors, Egyptians, the planets). One piece should have a good rhythmic sense with repeated clusters of phrases to convey an overall theme. The other should be random phrases that show no musical coherence.

What to do
Tell the children that they will be using the computer to compose their own music on a set topic (for example, space), applying repeated phrases throughout the composition with climaxes and areas of quiet. Show the class on a projector the basics of the composition software. Demonstrate to the children how to drag and drop the images on to the grid, how to alter the speed of the piece and how to delete phrases. Then play the two prepared pieces. Ask the children for their views. Discuss the key features of each example, pointing out the repeated clusters of sounds, the climax, whether there is coherence and so on.

Model the construction of the start of a new piece, drawing on the ideas that the children have already identified. Demonstrate how to repeat four, six or eight bars, possibly building tension or having a period of quiet. Give the children 15 minutes to produce the first 32 bars of their piece. Ask the children to use the headphones to facilitate independent work.

Review the children's work after 15 minutes drawing on good practice: what key features have the children included already? Give the children a further 25 minutes to finish their composition, again encouraging independence. To end the lesson, share one particularly good example of composition. Ask the children to pick out the key features of the piece. Invite other individuals to evaluate their own work. Did they manage to compose a build up of tension or a section of quiet calm? What aspect of the lesson was the most difficult?

Special support
Allow children their own headphones to work independently.

Extension
Use the program for children to compose a longer piece of music, or add music to a Powerpoint presentation.

AGE RANGE
Nine to eleven.

GROUP SIZE
Whole group.

LEARNING OBJECTIVE FOR ALL THE CHILDREN
● To add music and percussion to poetry and then perform.

INDIVIDUAL BEHAVIOUR TARGET
● To contribute new ideas with confidence.

Performance poetry

Poetry provides a way to help children with emotional difficulties express themselves appropriately.

What you need
Selection of musical instruments; pencils; Dictaphone or cassette and microphone to record the performance; large selection of poetry (for example, 'Jabberwocky' by Lewis Carroll, 'The Pied Piper of Hamelin' by Robert Browning, 'All in Time to the Music' and 'The Sound Collector' by Roger McGough, 'Night Mail' by WH Auden, 'The Owl and the Pussycat' by Edward Lear and 'An Ending' by Wendy Cope).

Preparation
Have multiple copies of the poetry available. Split the instruments up into group sets to provide each group with a set rather than allowing free selection.

What to do
Begin the lesson by reminding the children of poems they have read previously, perhaps in Literacy. Ask them to share ideas on their favourite poems and poets. What makes a poem a favourite? Select one poem from your list that can be read as a class. Initially discuss the poem generally, for example: the nonsense words in 'Jabberwocky' or the onomatopoeia in 'The Sound Collector'. Ask the children to suggest ways the poem can be enhanced using a variety of instruments.

Tell the children that they will be working in small groups to perform a poem to the class. Explain that they will be adding music to a poem of their choice either through sound effects, percussion or a melody. Split the class into groups of six to eight children, ensuring that each group has a mixed level of ability. Give the children five minutes initially to score their music around the poem, writing down all initial ideas. Ask one child in each group to feedback initial ideas to the whole class.

Give the children a set amount of time (for example, 30 minutes) to score and rehearse their poem. Circulate around the groups offering suggestions for improvements and encouraging all members to participate as fully as they can. To end the lesson, bring all of the groups together to be the audience. Ask each group in turn to perform their poem, recording their work on to cassette. At the end of each performance ask everyone to evaluate the work.

Special support
When you share ideas between groups, it may help children who are struggling by giving them additional ideas and choices.

Extension
Ask the children to add dramatic performance, costumes and so on to their poems, perhaps for a class assembly.

PHYSICAL EDUCATION

We are each of us different and you will have found that there are certain children whose behaviour definitely benefits from the chance to 'run off steam' and others who become immediately overexcited and out of control as soon as the adrenalin starts to flow. On balance, the benefits of PE far outweigh the 'risks'. You can use this curriculum strand to great advantage by helping the children with behavioural, emotional and social difficulties release emotions and stress appropriately. It can also form a useful part of a programme for stress and *anger management* for many of the children.

The key to successful lessons will lie in careful planning, keeping a 'flow' between activities, making them meaningful and motivating and knowing your children as individuals. You will need to use *clear rules* and, where possible, show children what to do as well as tell them. You might choose to warm up and then plan an energetic activity at the beginning of the lesson, or you might decide to build up to this gradually, so that it signals the end of the session. You might also need to plan carefully for any extra support assistance. Although children with learning difficulties are usually best supported in the more academic areas of the curriculum, you may have found that those with behaviour difficulties need more attention than usual when lessons are less structured and there are fewer physical boundaries. There are no hard-and-fast rules: use your observations to decide on the best way of planning PE lessons for the children in your class.

PE provides many opportunities for *shaping* up physical skills step by small step. Therefore, *chaining*, *personal best*, *rules-praise-ignore*, *targeted praise* and *ABC behaviour plans* can be very effective. Part of your planning will probably involve thinking about groupings, *separating the 'pack'* when you can and *avoiding situations* that are likely to cause problems. There are real chances for very active or disruptive children to achieve success in this strand and *build self-esteem*, so make use of *good role models*, *peer* and *spot praise*, *positive expectations*, *special responsibilities* and *positive affirmations*.

In order to maintain the flow, try to make use of approaches that allow you to note and respond to inappropriate behaviour without disrupting the whole lesson. These include *face-savers*, *hand signals*, *incompatible behaviours*, *take two*, *traffic lights*, the *'certain look'*, *humour*, *'when' statements* and the *count of three*. Give a *warning* before a change of activity or the end of the lesson, and focus certain children so that they round off what they are doing and move on. If a child is becoming overexcited or angry, use *deep breaths*, *nurture corners* or *time out* before trouble takes place rather than as a response to it.

In this section, you will find several activities that make use of a mixture of energetic and calming activities that are tightly structured and motivating. Try these lessons out and use them as a starting point for planning a wider range of PE activities based on what works best for the children in your class.

AGE RANGE
Five to seven.

GROUP SIZE
Whole class.

LEARNING OBJECTIVE FOR ALL THE CHILDREN
● To show an awareness of space and other children when playing a simple team game.

INDIVIDUAL BEHAVIOUR TARGET
● To become physically active without becoming angry or overexcited.

As quiet as mice

Children who are over-boisterous, angry or testing boundaries may become quickly out of control during physical activity. Here is a lesson that combines a tight structure with fun and plenty of activity, with the aim that the children know the boundaries and want to adhere to them.

What you need
Hall space; tambourine; yellow beanbags; four different coloured markers.

Preparation
Put a different coloured marker in each corner of the hall.

What to do
Tell the children that you are going to play a game called 'As quiet as mice'. Divide the class into four groups and position one group in each corner of the hall. The coloured markers will help younger children remember which corner their group is in.

Tell the children that they are all hungry mice who are afraid to come out of their mouse-holes because they have seen a cat prowling about outside.

Choose someone to be the cat. Whenever the cat goes to sleep, the mice can creep out of their mouse-holes to look for food. Emphasise the need to move as quietly as possible to avoid waking the cat. Should the cat wake up, signal this by beating the tambourine the mice must travel quickly back to their corners and curl up quietly on the floor. Anyone who gets caught by the cat is out of the game.

It is very easy for children to become overexcited and very noisy when playing a game like this. It is therefore important to have strategies in place for *targeted praise* throughout the game. This is where the yellow beanbags – the 'pieces of cheese' – come in. Reward those children who travel quietly back to their mouse-hole and curl up sensibly with a 'piece of cheese'.

At the end of the game, the winning group is the one that has collected the most yellow beanbags. Consider why this team won and highlight examples of appropriate behaviour.

Special support
Make use of *traffic lights* and *counts of three* to keep excitement levels down and add a *hand signal* if it helps to warn certain children they are going 'over the top'.

Extension
Try playing the game without the tambourine to encourage careful looking skills. Encourage the children to think of new and imaginative variations.

AGE RANGE
Five to seven.

GROUP SIZE
Whole class.

LEARNING OBJECTIVES FOR ALL THE CHILDREN
● To copy, remember and repeat simple actions with control and co-ordination.
● To create and perform a short sequence of actions with a partner.

INDIVIDUAL BEHAVIOUR TARGET
● To be confident enough to perform a linked sequence of movements in front of a large group.

Underwater patterns

Children who lack confidence in their ability to succeed will often become silly and disruptive rather than fail in front of others. Here is a lesson that guarantees success.

What you need
Hall space; a loosely-tied bundle of strips of different coloured crépe paper; simple pictures of fish and other underwater creatures, seaweed, rocks and shells; *Rainbow Fish* by Marcus Pfister (North–South Books).

Preparation
Read *Rainbow Fish* to the children as a stimulus for this lesson.

What to do
Play a game of 'Follow-my-leader' as a warm up. Pretend to be the Rainbow Fish by holding the crépe-paper tassels behind you to represent beautiful scales. Lead the rest of the group, varying the speed, level and direction of movements. Show the children the picture of a fish. Discuss how they could make their body shape like a fish and move like a fish. Have them try, and praise them. Repeat for other underwater creatures. For example:
Crab: move sideways low to the ground
Dolphin: travel quickly and gracefully on different levels
Jellyfish: dangle arms, travel on different levels turning slowly
Rocks and shells: curl up on the floor and be still
Seaweed: make a tall, spiky body shape.
Explain that you would like the children, in pairs, to devise a short sequence of underwater movements. The sequence must be made up of a 'movement–balance–movement', using the actions you have practised as a class, for example: 'fish–seaweed–jellyfish' or 'shark–rock–fish'. Tell the class at the end of the lesson that you are going to share your beautiful scales with children who work sensibly and perform a good sequence. Ask the children to find a partner. Allow time for them to devise and practise a sequence of movements with your suggestions and encouragement.
Gather the class together. Ask each pair of children to perform their sequence. After each performance, ask one child to say something they liked about it and pick the three picture cards that represent the movements used to create the sequence. If the correct pictures can be identified, award the performers a 'scale'. Finish with 'Follow-my-leader' with all the children carrying their tassel.

Special support
Shape the behaviour by expecting a sequence of two to begin with.

Extension
Design an underwater dance to music, combining all your patterns and sequences.

AGE RANGE
Seven to nine.

GROUP SIZE
Whole class.

LEARNING OBJECTIVE FOR ALL THE CHILDREN
● To use the tactic of finding space in a competitive game.

INDIVIDUAL BEHAVIOUR TARGET
● To find a space and not to invade the space of others.

Basketball

Children who lack self-control find it very hard to find their own space and not be distracted by the proximity of other active children.

What you need
Adequate space; basketballs; hoops (or a chair as a goal); bibs or bands for teams; cones to separate basketball courts; stopwatch.

Preparation
The children should have some knowledge of basketball and other invasion games before this lesson. Ensure the space is free from hazards and safe for the children to run around in.

What to do
Begin the lesson by warming the children up with a game of 'Tail tag'. Give each child a band and ask them to tuck it into their waistbands or pockets with a tail hanging down behind them. Select about five children to be 'on'. Explain that upon your signal the five children will try to collect as many tails as they can in 60 seconds. Count the children down from five, and time one minute. Ask them to sit down and count how many tails have been collected. Evaluate who was successful and discuss what tactics they used. Select new tail-collectors and begin again. Evaluate once more and end the warm-up session with some stretches.

Ask the children to sit alongside one of the basketball courts. Remind the children that in 'Tail tag' they needed to find space and to be able to quickly change direction. Ask for four children to quickly demonstrate finding space and changing direction around the hall. Invite the children to suggest any good tips, for example: looking where you are going and changing direction by pivoting on one foot.

Demonstrate these skills with a game where four children are on the offensive with control of the ball and are attempting to score goals, and two children are trying to defend. Split the children up into groups and ask them to play using this 4:2 ratio. Give each group a small court, using the cones if necessary. Rotate the players so that each child has a turn attacking and defending.

After approximately 15 minutes, bring all the children together again and review the skills so far. Ask the children to finish with a cool down. Ensure the children are calm and relaxed before they leave the hall.

Special support
Separate the *'pack'* if there is a group of disruptive children and make use of *good role models.*

Extension
Move on to more evenly matched games of seven children a side.

AGE RANGE
Seven to nine.

GROUP SIZE
Whole class.

LEARNING OBJECTIVE FOR ALL THE CHILDREN
● To know and understand their own bodies.

INDIVIDUAL BEHAVIOUR TARGET
● To learn a simple relaxation technique.

Relaxation games

Children who are very active or impulsive are particularly challenged by having to keep still, yet this is an important part of relaxation. Here are ideas for making quiet and calm moments motivating too and helping children to listen to signals in their bodies.

Draining energy
What you need
Mats or cushions for the children to lie on.

What to do
Tell the children to lie on their backs in spaces around the hall. Ask them to close their eyes. Explain that you will try to help them to relax their whole bodies and minds. Tell them to imagine that their bodies are full of yellow liquid and that this represents the energy they are all full of. Down by their toes is the tap and you are going to drain all of the energy from their bodies. Talk the children through this process, starting from the toes and working up the body to the head. For example: 'Feel the energy draining from your toes, feel your ankles becoming relaxed. This process should take about ten minutes to travel from the tips of the toes to the top of the head. As you reach the top of the head, tell the children to try to clear their minds, give them a few moments of silence to complete the relaxation session.

Musical relaxation
What you need
CD or cassette player; familiar, relaxing music; gym mats.

What to do
Tell the children how long the piece of music is and explain that they have that long to relax completely – if they can! Ask the children to begin sitting up with their eyes closed. Explain that the music will get quieter and quieter and as this happens the children must try more and more to relax completely. Tell them that they can lie down in whatever position is comfortable in order to relax completely. When the children are quiet and ready, begin the music. Approximately every 30 seconds turn the music down gradually. Towards the end of the track fade the volume down to nothing and wait in silence for a few moments. In a quiet voice tell the children the session is over and that when they are ready they should sit up.

Special support
These exercises can form part of a stress or *anger management* technique. Use of *deep breaths* and *visualisation* as well.

Extension
Discuss what happened to the children as they became relaxed.

AGE RANGE
Nine to eleven.

GROUP SIZE
Whole class.

LEARNING OBJECTIVE FOR ALL THE CHILDREN
● To understand and participate in group games effectively.

INDIVIDUAL BEHAVIOUR TARGET
● To move safely at speed.

Fast games

Some children with behavioural difficulties benefit from 'letting off steam' at the beginning or end of a PE lesson.

Fruit basket
What you need
Large space, indoors or out.

What to do
Ask the children to sit in a large circle, well spaced out. Give each child the name of a fruit (for example, apple, orange, banana, grape). Explain that the name of a fruit will be shouted out and that the children who are that fruit must stand up, run around the circle in a clockwise direction and return to sit in their place. Practise this. Tell the children that the last person to return to their seat will be out and will have to sit in the centre of the circle. After the first few turns add an extra complication: when 'fruit basket' is shouted out, all fruits must run around the circle clockwise and then return to their seats. This can be quite chaotic and the children need to be aware of their own space as well as others as they run. Tell the children they should look where they are going and they should move at a safe speed. The fruit theme can be varied to fit in with the interests of the children in your class (for example, sports cars, television programmes and pop stars).

Wacky relay races
What you need
Field or playground with lanes marked for running (about a 15m track); stickers for winners; hoops, cones, skipping ropes, balls – any resources that can add a little fun!

What to do
Organise the children into teams of four or five seated behind their first runner at the start line. Explain that they will be running a variety of relay races up to the halfway line and back again. The second runner will start as the first returns to the starting line and so on. Take yourself to the halfway stage, where the children will be turning around, and marshal the race from there. Give the children an official: 'On your marks, get set, go!'. Continue with variations which could include: skipping to the halfway point and running back; skipping with a hula hoop to the halfway line and jogging back; dribbling a basketball there and bouncing it back again.

Special support
Use *clear rules*, *targeted praise* and *peer praise*. If children become overexcited, give *warnings* and use *time out* for *deep breaths*.

Extension
Encourage children to invent variations on these themes.

AGE RANGE
Nine to eleven.

GROUP SIZE
Whole class.

LEARNING OBJECTIVE FOR ALL THE CHILDREN
● To record their own performance and to set personal targets for the future.

INDIVIDUAL BEHAVIOUR TARGET
● To become self-motivated to exercise regularly.

Circuit training

There are long-term benefits for children in having regular exercise and developing fitness – this is especially true for children who find it hard to control their adrenalin flow and emotions.

What you need
Benches, skipping ropes, tennis balls and rackets; cones or markers to separate the areas of the hall; score sheets and pencils – one per child; stopwatch.

Preparation
Set out the equipment and instructions in the hall to facilitate six different activities, for example: step-ups, star jumps, continual skipping, squat thrusts, bouncing a tennis ball on a racket and sprinting one side of the hall. Prepare score sheets that can be used over several weeks, including sections for setting future targets and recording scores.

What to do
Share the objective with the children – that they will be recording their own performance and setting targets for future achievement. Remind them of the importance of a good warm up. Ask volunteers to lead groups of five or six children through the warm up. Children will respond well to the responsibility and it will keep them focused.

Walk the class around the hall, showing them each activity in turn. Explain that they will have 60 seconds to complete as many of each exercise as possible in the time. Ask one or two children to demonstrate good practice for each exercise (for example, straight arms on star jumps or bringing the feet right in close to the hands on squat thrusts). Show the children the appropriate place on the worksheet to fill in their scores. Make sure they understand that they will be improving their scores over the next few weeks, so they should not compare themselves with others – the only score they need to beat is their own!

Split the children into groups of approximately five and work with one group yourself. Send the children off to their starting activity. Count the children down from five for their first exercise minute. At the end of this time, ask the children to share their achievements – begin with your group as this will be an honest benchmark. Then let the children log their scores on to their sheet.

Special support
This activity lends itself to the use of *personal best*, *self-monitoring* and a *consequences approach*.

Extension
Consider other ways of establishing exercise regimes and encourage children to pursue a long-term personal exercise plan.

RECOMMENDED RESOURCES

HELPFUL READING

- *Effective Intervention in Primary Schools – Nurture Groups* by M Bennathan and M Boxhall (David Fulton Publishers).
- DfEE and QCA: *The National Curriculum: Handbook for primary teachers in England Key Stages 1 and 2.*
- DfEE: *The National Numeracy Strategy.*
- DfES: *Promoting Children's Mental Health within Early Years and School Settings.*
- DfES: *Special Educational Needs Code of Practice* (ref DfES 581/2001).
- DfES: *The National Literacy Strategy* and *Early Literacy Support Programme.*
- DfES: *The National Literacy and Numeracy Strategies: Including All Children in the Literacy Hour and Daily Mathematics Lesson.*
- *Managing Behaviour in the Primary School* by J Docking (David Fulton Publishers).
- *Anger Management: A Practical Guide* by A Faupel, E Herrick and P Sharp (David Fulton Publishers).
- *Spotlight on Special Educational Needs: Emotional and Behavioural Difficulties* by J Fogell and R Long (NASEN).
- *Beyond Toddlerdom – Keeping Five-to Twelve-year-olds on the Rails* by C Green (Vermilion).
- *Circle of Friends and Promoting Self-esteem* by Jackie Lown (Positive Behaviour Management at 7 Quinton Close, Ainsdale, Merseyside, PR8 2TD).

- *The No-blame Approach* by B Maines and G Robinson (Lucky Duck Publishing).
- *Behavioural and Emotional Difficulties* by H Mortimer, from the *Special Needs in the Early Years* series (Scholastic).
- *Developing Individual Behaviour Plans in Early Years Settings* by H Mortimer (NASEN).
- *Turn Your School Around* and *Quality Circle Time in the Primary Classroom* by J Mosley (LDA).
- *Supporting Children with Behaviour Difficulties* by G Fox (David Fulton Publishers).
- *Plans for Better Behaviour in the Primary School – Management and Intervention* by S Roffey and T O'Reirdan (David Fulton Publishers).
- *Nurturing Emotional Literacy* by P Sharp (David Fulton Publishers).
- *Effective Teaching and Learning in the Classroom – A Practical Guide to Brain Compatible Learning* by Sara Shaw and Trevor Hawes (Optimal Learning series Leicester: The SERVICES Ltd).
- *Helping Families with Troubled Children – A Preventative Approach* by C Sutton (Wiley).
- *How to Promote Children's Social and Emotional Competence* by C Webster-Stratton (Paul Chapman Publishing).

USEFUL RESOURCES

- **Being Yourself** (hand puppets and therapeutic games for professionals working to improve mental well-being and emotional literacy in children) – send for a catalogue from The Old Bakery, Charlton House, Dour Street, Dover, CT16 1ED. Website: www.smallwood.co.uk.
- **Brainwaves** (reward sticker albums and so on), Bodwin, Cornwall, PL31 2RT.
- **LDA**, Primary and Special Needs, Duke Street, Wisbech, Cambridgeshire PE13 2AE. Tel: 01945 46344. Supplies *Circle Time Kit* by Jenny Moseley (puppets, rainstick, magician's cloak and many props for making circle time motivating).

● **Lucky Duck Publishing Ltd** – send for a catalogue of videos, books and resources. Tel: 0117-9732881. Website: www.luckyduck.co.uk.

● **Magination Press** specialises in books which help young children deal with personal or psychological concerns. Send for a catalogue from The Eurospan Group, 3 Henrietta Street, Covent Garden, London WC2E 8LU. www.maginationpress.com.

● **Positive Parenting** booklets in three age ranges: Managing your four- to eight-year-old, Managing your eight- to 12-year-old and Managing your 13- to 16-year-old by Stockton-on-Tees Educational Psychology Service (QEd).

● Super Stickers (for reward and motivation) from PO Box 55, 4 Balloo Ave, Bangor, County Down BT19 7PJ. Tel: 028 9145 4344.

● The *Understanding Childhood* leaflets are available from **The Child Psychotherapy Trust**, Star House, 104–108 Grafton Road, London NW5 4BD. Send for a catalogue.

● **Speechmark Publishing Ltd**, Telford Road, Bicester, Oxford OX26 4LQ.

Freephone (UK) 0800 243755 (send for their catalogue of books to help children with feelings).

● **Winslow**, Goyt Side Road, Chesterfield, Derbyshire S40 2PH. www.winslow-cat.com (send for their 'extra' catalogue which covers self-esteem, emotional literacy, anger management, behaviour development, bullying, bereavement and loss and multi-cultural society).

● **nfer Nelson**: www.nfer-nelson.co.uk (send for a catalogue of assessment resources).

● **The Psychological Corporation**, Harcourt Education, Halley Court, Jordan Hill, Oxford OX2 8EJ. www.tpc-international.com (send for their catalogue on 'Educational Assessment & Intervention').

● **Don Johnston Special Needs**, 18/19 Clarendon Court, Calver Road, Winwick Quay, Warrington WA2 8QP. www.donjohnston.com (send for their catalogue on IT solutions for special needs).